IT HAPPENED IN
PENNSYLVANIA

Fran Capo and Scott Bruce

TWODOT®

GUILFORD, CONNECTICUT
HELENA, MONTANA
AN IMPRINT OF THE GLOBE PEQUOT PRESS

A · T W O D O T® · B O O K

Copyright © 2005 by The Globe Pequot Press

Map by Sue Cary

Library of Congress Cataloging-in-Publication Data
Capo, Fran, 1959-
  It happened in Pennsylvania / Fran Capo and Scott Bruce.— 1st ed.
     p. cm. — (It happened in series)
  Includes bibliographical references (p.) and index.
  ISBN 0-7627-3046-3
  1. Pennsylvania—History—Anecdotes. I. Bruce, Scott, 1954- II. Title.
     III. Series.
  F149.6.C37 2005
  974.8—dc22

                                                2005040311

Manufactured in the United States of America
First Edition/First Printing

To my son, Spencer; my mom, Rose; my fiancé, Steve;
and my friend Andy Scarpati of Comedy Cabaret . . .
all people with whom I have shared many fond
memories of Pennsylvania.
—Fran

To Anne, Nick, Chloe, and especially Rob.
—Scott

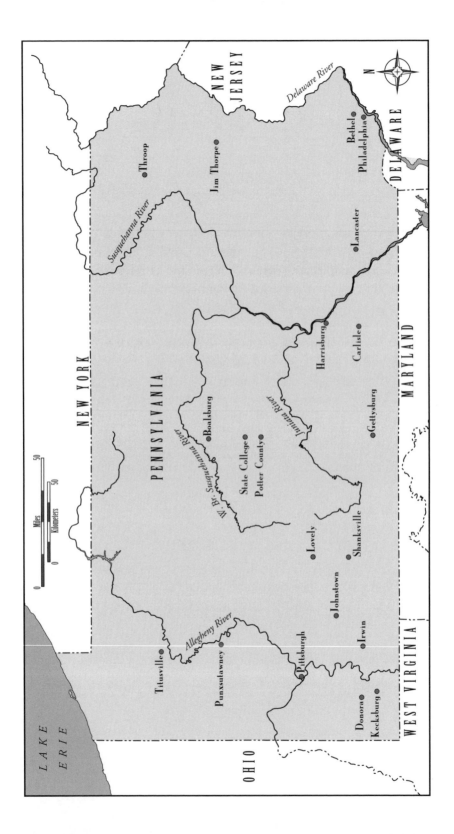

Contents

Preface

When I first wrote *It Happened in New York*, I made a deal with Globe Pequot that if the book did well, I could go on to write *It Happened in New Jersey*. Well, thanks to you, dear reader, it did well and I wrote it. I put the same detective work into that book as my first, researching the hard-to-find facts that, to me, make history come alive. Little did I know this would start a trend and I would be asked to write this book, *It Happened in Pennsylvania*. At first I said no, remembering all the hard labor that goes into each one of these slim tomes. But then I remembered a conversation I had at a comedy club one night with a fellow comedian, Scott Bruce. He had read my other books and said, "If you ever decide to write something on Pennsylvania, I'd love to be included." You see, besides being a stand-up comic, Scott was also hosting a television show called *The Pennsylvania Game*, so it seemed like a natural fit; plus, let's face it, it would be half the work. I introduced him to my publisher and the rest is history. This is Scott's first book, and so I hope you welcome him into your homes as you have done with me. When people collaborate they have to try to keep the writing voice as one. We have tried hard to do that, taking into account that we are both strong-willed people. So hopefully you will not sit there and think Scott's chapter, Fran's chapter, Scott's chapter, Fran's chapter. Although that in itself can make a cute trivia game.

Before I turn this over to Scott, I want to say one more thing. There are many chapters we wanted to include in this book but were unable to. For example, we wanted to include a chapter on the birth of the Marines but discovered that there wasn't enough information about Tun Tavern, its birthplace. We also felt it was essential to include a chapter on the Amish. Unfortunately, since they are a very private people, the only real information we found was an incident in the paper on the only Amish murder. Since we didn't want to focus on this peaceful group's one blemish, we left the chapter out. Scott and I chose chapters that we thought would be diverse enough to whet the appetites of all our readers and, as is always a goal of mine, put in information that would have even the historians saying, "Wow, I didn't know that!"

And now before I write the whole introduction myself, I'd like to introduce my partner in crime, Scott Bruce. Lights go up, Scott takes the stage.

Wow!!! These lights are bright! I think we can attribute the extra wattage to Fran Capo. When Fran proposed the idea of working together on this book, I thought she was taking a pretty big leap of faith. After all, I had never written anything on this scale. Fortunately Fran knew of my interest in the subject matter: I love Pennsylvania and I love history. While I may have had few difficulties in finding material that I wanted to write about, I must stress the important role Fran had in helping me to understand the process of writing.

The most important point I can convey here is how much I have enjoyed this endeavor. The sweat and effort involved in producing this work is easily eclipsed by the joy this project has brought to me personally. My only hope is that you, the reader, have even a small amount of that joy in the reading.

From both of us to you—happy reading!

Acknowledgments

We would like to thank our editor, Stephanie, for working with us quickly on the chapters.

Fran would like to thank:

Once again, as with all my books, my son, Spencer; my mom, Rose; and fiancé, Steve, who all were willing to share my time by letting me work endlessly on this book.

My son, Spencer, who let me read every single chapter to him to get the teenage stamp of approval that they were interesting.

Marian Yevics and Mary Ann Moran, research assistant and executive director of the Lackawanna Historical Society, respectively, for sending me the copies of the newspaper accounts of the Throop mining disaster. The info was here before I could dry the stamp on my envelope. Thanks guys, for being so efficient and prompt!

Bob Currin of the Potter County Historical Society, for helping with the information on Dr. Bentley.

Bob Beck of the Gulf Oil Historical Society, for all his amusing and informative e-mails on the first service station.

Scott Wedgbury of the International Revolving Door Association. Scott led me to a diary of Van Kennel, the man who invented the revolving door, but I couldn't find the inspiration in Kennel's diary that led to the invention, so the chapter was dropped. But I still thank Scott for his time.

Marilyn Holt of the Carnegie Library in Pittsburgh, for sending me the photocopied articles on the Flatheads gang.

Miss Ellen at the Doylestown library, for leading me to information on Three Mile Island.

Lou Harry, a fellow comedian and author, who gave me a great lead to call the Temple University Library to find out more unique stories on Pennsylvania.

Michael French, the communication director at the Walnut Street Theater, who desperately tried to help me find more information on a stagehand who willed his skull to the theater. Unfortunately, I wasn't able to find enough information to write a full chapter.

Scott would like to thank:

My wife, Anne; son, Nicholas; and daughter, Chloe, all of whom gave me the space and encouragement to undertake something new.

Fran Capo for her guidance and patience.

All my brothers and sisters: Kathy, Betsy, Tom, Joan, Luann, and especially Rob, who was my inspiration.

My parents, Dick and Gloria, who provided firsthand information for much of this work.

Patty Satalia, the producer of *The Pennsylvania Game* TV show on PBS. Patty opened her research files for me, lent me books, and provided inside information that proved to be invaluable.

Richard Burkert, the executive director of the Johnstown Flood Museum, as well as Helen Boemmel and all the tour guides who put up with all my questions and queries.

Barbara Zolli, the director of the Drake Oil Well Museum, and Linda Riccardo, who provided key information on the subject.

Roberta Dinsmore of the Punxsutawney Memorial Library, also known as "the keeper" of Punxsutawney Phil, legendary weather prognosticator.

Thomas E. and Betty Lou McBride, for their admirable work in keeping up the Old Jail Museum in Jim Thorpe, Pennsylvania. Their tour guides are top notch and my visit was fun and informative.

A special thanks to whomever invented the Internet.

And finally to all the staff of the Hazleton Area Public Library. Many thanks for putting up with my unending questions. Special thanks to Mr. Neopolitan and Mrs. Dougherty in the reference department, James Reimiller for running a wonderful operation, and Ruth Ann Generose for help with computers, copiers, and being an all-around good egg.

A Witch in Pennsylvania

· 1683 ·

Whenever the words "witch trial" are mentioned, Salem, Massachusetts, quickly comes to mind. But the "demons" of that time were tried in other states as well, and Pennsylvania was no exception. The first and only witch trial in Pennsylvania took place in Bethel Township on December 21, 1683. However, unlike most of the Salem trials, this one had a much brighter ending.

There was a law in existence at the time that had carried over from the days of Britain's King James I, which stated it was illegal to commit "conjuration, witchcraft and dealing with evil and wicked spirits." However, this law was wide open to interpretation. And so the day came when Margaret Mattson, a native of Sweden, was accused of being a witch and of having malignant and evil powers. The colonists feared her, and she was brought to trial in front of both a jury and a panel of judges, which was led by none other than Governor William Penn himself, for whom the state would later be named. Penn didn't want any riffraff in his colony and so he took this case very seriously. However, he was also a man of law, and he made certain all of the evidence was weighed.

According to the *Minutes of the Provincial Council of Pennsylvania,* several witnesses were called during the trial.

First on the stand was Henry Drystreet. Drystreet told of an unusual series of events.

> He was tould 20 years agoe, that the prisoner (Mattson) at the barr was a witch and that several cows were bewitcht by her; also, that James Sanderling's mother told him that she bewitcht her cow, but afterwards said it was a mistake, and that her cow should do well again, for it was not her cow but another person's that should dye.

Penn nodded and the next witness, Charles Ashcom, was called to the stand. Charles also had an interesting account to report.

> Anthony's wife being asked why she sold her cattle saith it was because her mother (Mattson) had bewitcht them, having taken the witchcraft of Hendrick's cattle, and also that one night the daughter of the prisoner called him up hastely, and when he came she sayd there was a great light but just before, and an old woman with a knife in her hand was at ye bedd's feet, and therefore she cryed out and desired Jno Symcock to take away his calves or else she would send them to Hell.

The only information the jury was able to gather from this confusing story was that Mattson's daughter had called Charles to come over because she had been frightened by a great light and an old woman with a knife at the foot of her bed. Supposedly that person was her mother in the midst of some bewitching act.

A few more witnesses gave their testimony, and then the final witness, Annakay Coolin, was called to add her account.

Her husband took the heart of a calfe that dyed, as they thought, by witchcraft, and boyled it, whereupon the prisoner at ye Barr came in and asked them what they were doing; they said boyling the flesh; she said they had better they had boyled the bones with several other unseemly expressions.

After all the testimony was heard, Penn turned to Margaret Mattson and asked her how she pled. According to the minutes, "The Prisoner denyeth all things, And saith that ye Witnesses speake only by hear say."

Penn then turned to the grand jury and read the charge against her again, which stated that she was in violation of the law of King James I, and that cattle were in grave danger. He then instructed them to return with a verdict.

Fortunately for Margaret, John Gibbons was on the jury. Gibbons lived on a large tract of land in Bethel and was the founder of one of the largest and most respected families of the old county of Chester. He was a very well-educated man, far brighter than most of his neighbors and fellow jurors. Because what jurors say occurs behind closed doors, no one will ever know what truly transpired. But it is reported that it was Gibbons's logic that convinced the jury to come back with a compromise verdict that would keep both the court and Mattson happy. The returned verdict prevented a long debate and disagreement among the members of the jury, saved Mattson's life, and secured her from having to face the ordeal of a second trial.

The verdict delivered in the courtroom on that December day stated that Margaret Mattson was "guilty of having the common fame of a witch, but not guilty in the manner and form as she stands indicted." Talk about a compromise!

The sentence? Fifty pounds to be paid by Mattson in order to guarantee her good behavior for the next six months. The case was adjourned, and no trouble was ever recorded on the books again for Margaret Mattson. Thus there was a happy ending for the one and only witch trial in the annals of Pennsylvania history.

For Whom the Bell Cracked

· 1752 ·

The great, impressive bell weighed over a ton. It stood a full 3 feet in height, was an astounding 12 feet in circumference at the lip, and held a forty-four-pound clapper. It had just arrived from England via boat and had been carefully carted from the Delaware River port in Philadelphia to the Pennsylvania State House. This government building was to be its new home. The bell tower had already been constructed and simply sat, awaiting the bell, but the decision was made to hang the bell on special trusses in the yard for a test ringing before it was permanently placed. Knowing the amount of effort that goes into raising a one-ton metal bell, no one wanted to position the bell on high only to learn it had a defect. After carefully securing the bell in its temporary home, an unknown worker was given the honor and privilege of striking the clapper to the bell—and to everyone's dismay, the great bell cracked!

The total useful life of this expensive grand bell in its current form was zip, nada, zilch, none. More than a year had gone into the planning, the ordering, the manufacturing, the shipping, and all the preparations, yet the device was now incapable of performing the only function that was required of it.

Imagine, if possible, how awful that worker felt at that moment when he realized the bell had cracked. Indeed, we probably can't conceive of the significance of the bell, for it was to be the primary source of announcements for the entire city of Philadelphia. Mass communication at the time was rather limited, and the big bell had been intended to gather the people for church services and important town meetings, to announce the death of a citizen, and as a call for help in the event of an emergency such as fire. In those days the sophisticated varieties of styles in the ringing could convey different meanings so people immediately understood the message the tolling carried. For instance, the distinctive death toll was customized to convey whether the deceased was male or female. Furthermore, the emergency ring could define the emergency as a fire, for example, as well as provide a pretty good idea where it was located. This insured that the people responding to the emergency could rush to the scene with a minimum of chaos. The bell had a second purpose in this new land as well. It was meant to represent and memorialize the Charter of Liberation of 1701. This charter had produced a stable government for the past fifty years.

What were the state and city officials to do about the cracked bell? They knew it could take another year to acquire a new bell from the mother country, since professional foundries with the laborers skilled enough to manufacture such a fine and enormous piece were few and far between. The first move would have to be to find out who might be at fault. A letter was sent on the first vessel back to England to inform the Whitechapel Foundry, manufacturer of the bell, of the possible defect. The Whitechapel Foundry, located in London's East End, was and is to this day one of the premier foundries in the world. When informed of the problem, they were outrageously offended. Their immediate reply was "no way!" These were proud craftsmen who took great pride in their product. They were of the opinion that the person who first rang the bell must have held the clapper to the body after the strike. This would have caused a huge vibration capable of creating the crack.

The current belief is that the answer lay somewhere in between the making and the ringing of the bell, literally! The facts show that the ocean voyage that carried the bell to North America was a very tempestuous ride. The ship logs indicate that there was substantial rough weather and the ship took more time in the crossing than was usual. The consensus is that the bell could easily have been knocked around on the ship, causing a hairline crack. Certainly no crack was detected on arrival, but a well-constructed bell, even one of this magnitude, is a very fragile instrument. Even the slightest defect caused by an untimely bump could have ultimately been the culprit.

The bottom line for the Pennsylvanians was that it would fall to them to repair or rebuild the bell. They looked no further than their own backyard. The team of John Pass and John Stow were engaged to rebuild the bell. Pass and Stow had foundry training and experience but were considered poor replacements for the famed Whitechapel Foundry. The need for frugality, however, led to the use of these novice craftsmen, and the cost of materials was prohibitive so the original bell was melted down. Pass and Stow took every precaution to duplicate the appearance of Whitechapel's initial creation, even matching the inscription exactly.

The inscription, and how it may have come to be, adds even more to the legend and importance of this bell in our nation's history. The speaker of the Assembly of Pennsylvania, Isaac Norris, sent a letter dated November 1, 1751, to Robert Charles, Pennsylvania's representative in London, requesting "a good bell of about two thousand pounds." Norris further stated that "the bell be cast by the best workmen and examined carefully before it is shipped." Speaker Norris also instructed that the bell be inscribed, reading "By order of the Assembly of the Province of Pensylvania [sic] for the State House in the City of Philadelphia, 1752" and below that, "Proclaim Liberty thro' all the land to all the inhabitants Thereof—Levit, XXV 10."

However, many scholars believe that Ben Franklin had a heavy hand in the creation of the inscription. While Norris was known for his straightforward and businesslike approach in letters and manner, Franklin was known far and wide as a philosopher and free thinker. Ben was also fond of quoting the Bible and insinuating his beliefs into any and all of his writings.

The other notable item in the inscription as laid out in Norris's letter is the misspelling of Pennsylvania, using just one "n." Clearly Isaac's letter shows the misspelling, and it could have been a simple mistake. However, the spelling of the word *Pennsylvania* was not yet standardized by 1750, and it is possible that Norris thought he was spelling it correctly. Either way, Pass and Stow dutifully reproduced the bell with the original spelling, as can be seen today.

Unfortunately the new bell as cast by Pass and Stow did not ring true either, so to speak. A great party was set up for the unveiling of the newest incarnation of the bell, and it took only one ring of this bell for all to realize that its unpleasant sound would not be acceptable. In fact one listener likened it to "the sound of two coal scuttles banged together." Wasting no time at all, Pass and Stow immediately went back to work. This time the artisans added more American copper to the mix along with some extra silver in hopes of sweetening the sound. Their second attempt met with success; nonetheless, the new and improved bell was introduced with little fanfare.

The *Pennsylvania Gazette* mentioned the final hanging of the bell in its June 7, 1753, issue, stating that "Last week was raised and fix'd in the Statehouse Steeple, the new great Bell, cast here by Pass and Stow, weighing 2080 lb with this Motto, Proclaim Liberty throughout the land unto all the inhabitants thereof; Lev. XXV 10."

While Pass and Stow made some corrections to the wording of the Bible passage and took liberty with the abbreviation of Leviticus to simply Lev., they did not make any changes to the spelling of Pennsylvania.

From these humble beginnings grew the legend and fame of our national symbol, the Liberty Bell. The bell was rung to herald the reading of the Declaration of Independence, as well as for many important community announcements over the years. It was moved when the British invaded, to prevent the enemy from melting it down to make ammunition. Hidden in the basement of a church in Allentown, it was returned to the state house after the Torries were swept out of Philadelphia.

On July 8, 1835, the old bell failed again, cracking as it tolled for the passing of the Chief Justice of the United States, John Marshall. There are only two more recorded instances of use of the bell after this crack. The bell was muffled and tolled for the death of President William Henry Harrison in 1841, and five years later, after attempts were made at repairs, it was rung in 1846 to celebrate George Washington's birthday. After this event the bell was officially retired.

Ironically, the first reference to the bell as the "Liberty Bell" came not from Philadelphia but from a pamphlet produced in Boston. Furthermore, the liberty that was referred to was not religious or political, as it originally had been; it was used in a pamphlet supporting freedom for African Americans from slavery. The pamphlet was distributed in 1839 by a group called the "Friends of Freedom" and featured a drawing of the old bell with its now-famous inscription and the caption "Liberty Bell." The idea that the Liberty Bell represented freedom and liberty not just for slaves but for all Americans caught on with the general public. Through the years the bell became one of our country's most important symbols representing these values.

Today the Liberty Bell stands just inside the doors of Independence Hall in Philadelphia. This has been its home since 1915, and thousands of people visit it daily. The defective bell that made its first appearance in America way back in 1752 will remain here to remind us of this permanent "crack" in time.

The Birth of a Nation
· 1776 ·

On the 4th of July in 1776, the representatives of the thirteen original British colonies of North America met in Philadelphia and decided on a name change. They would now refer to their nation as the United States of America. Of course this was not a change in name only. This was in word and on paper a declaration of independence from the tyrannical rule of King George III.

Most Americans know the facts of this story. However there is another story from the times that reveals a different twist. Our Independence Day could very well be celebrated on the second of July each year instead of the fourth. It is also possible that the document associated with this independence could be something more prosaically called the Lee Resolution.

On June 7, 1776, an unmistakable cry for independence was made at the meeting of the second Continental Congress in Philadelphia. At that assembly Richard Henry Lee of Virginia read this resolution, known simply as the Lee Resolution, to be voted upon before our founding fathers.

> Resolved: That these United Colonies are, and of right ought to be, free and independent States, that they are absolved from all allegiance to the British Crown, and that all political connection between them and the State of Great Britain is, and ought to be, totally dissolved.

This resolution was short, sweet, and to the point, making clear the fact that the people of the thirteen colonies were very upset with their political situation. The second Continental Congress was the only acting government that represented the people. Obviously the Parliament of England was unresponsive to the grievances of the colonies. Complaints of taxation without representation as well as a heavy-handed governing style had gone on for years with little or no redress from the crown.

At this time there were still some delegates who were not ready to commit to severing all ties with England. It was determined that a break of three weeks was needed for members to go home and gather information from the people they represented. When the Congress reconvened on July 1, they would plan to vote on the Lee Resolution. The overall feeling among these politicians was that the resolution would pass at that time.

Before the recess however, one more item was added to their agenda. It was decided that a committee of five members would draft a more formidable announcement than the Lee Resolution. This would be a proclamation to the world that would explain the colonies' justification for independence.

The committee was comprised of two members from New England, two members from the middle colonies, and one member representing the South. They were future president John Adams of Massachusetts, Roger Sherman of Connecticut, Benjamin Franklin of Pennsylvania, Robert Livingston of New York, and another future president, Thomas Jefferson of Virginia. In a separate vote, the committee elected Thomas Jefferson to write the original draft. The idea was that he would prepare the document and then present it to the rest of the committee for approval before the second Continental Congress reconvened.

When Jefferson completed a first draft, he provided copies for both Franklin and Adams, asking them for corrections and other input. The revised document went to the committee of five and from there it would be passed, unaltered, to the Congress.

July 1 brought the Continental Congress back into session. The important vote on Lee's Resolution was scheduled for July 2. Twelve of the thirteen colonies took part in the vote, with New York abstaining. All twelve voted in favor of the resolution for independence as proposed by Richard Henry Lee. Discussions and debate began immediately about Thomas Jefferson's Declaration of Independence, but the fact is that the Continental Congress had already declared independence from Great Britain by accepting Lee's Resolution. Jefferson's document would simply be the public announcement of what had already been decided.

July 2 is the official day that the United States of America was born! How would you like to find out that you spent your entire life celebrating the wrong birthday? Why did our founding fathers choose the fourth over the second? Why did they choose Jefferson's Declaration of Independence over Lee's Resolution? The answer is that they did not. At least some members, including John Adams of Massachusetts, believed that July 2 was our nation's Independence Day. The fact that Congress was still in session and had more legislation to deal with made resolving the issue of the actual date seem like a small matter. What was extremely important was gaining agreement on the words of the actual public document that would explain to the world what was going on in the North American colonies.

The debate on the Jefferson document continued for two more days. There were a few additions and deletions, but the original manuscript survived with very few changes. Late in the day on Thursday, the 4th of July, church bells rang out all over the city of Philadelphia. The Declaration of Independence had been officially approved. Printers were assigned the task of duplicating the Declaration of Independence for distribution to the heads of the states. This document, with its concise wording that so fully described the feelings and beliefs of the people it represented, was chosen to be the symbol of the brand new United States of America.

A formal ceremonial announcement was held outside of the state house on Monday, July 8, at noon. Word passed quickly through the countryside. Messengers to all parts of what could now be called the United States of America brought the exciting news of the birth of a new nation. Monday morning turned out to be the perfect day for this grand unveiling. It was a beautiful summer day. A special stage was built on the lawn of the state house, and every bell in the area tolled to assemble the townspeople for the reading of the Declaration of Independence. Many had gathered early in the day in the festive manner of a picnic.

Just before noon a tall gentleman by the name of Colonel John Nixon climbed the steps to the platform. (It should be noted that even though President Richard Milhous Nixon could trace his family tree all the way back to revolutionary times, he was not related to this Colonel John Nixon.) The colonel quieted the crowd and began to read.

IN CONGRESS, July 4, 1776.

The unanimous Declaration of the thirteen united States of America,

When in the Course of human events, it becomes necessary for one people to dissolve the political bands which have connected them with another, and to assume among the powers of the earth, the separate and equal station to which the Laws of Nature and of Nature's God entitle them, a decent respect to the opinions of mankind requires that they should declare the causes which impel them to the separation.

We hold these truths to be self-evident, that all men are created equal, that they are endowed by their Creator with certain unalienable Rights, that among these are Life, Liberty and the pursuit of Happiness.

He continued to read the declaration in its entirety as the crowd listened intently. The eloquence of these words, along with the deep meaning behind them, is enough for any of us to see why we chose this document, signed on the 4th of July, to indicate the true birth of our nation, with apologies to Richard Henry Lee and his resolution.

Still, the mystery remains as to exactly why the country chose to celebrate on the 4th. The case has been made that July 2nd is the anniversary of the birth of our nation, and that July 8th is the anniversary of the public announcement. Here's a thought: Why not celebrate all three days?

Up, Up, and Away!
· 1793 ·

In the early morning of January 9, 1793, forty thousand spectators anxiously waited outside the walls of the Walnut Street Prison, ready to witness a great event. Since 6:00 that morning, loud booms from two artillery pieces positioned at Potter's Field went off every fifteen minutes to remind those still sleeping to get out of bed and hurry to the streets. The city had been talking about it for weeks. What was it? No, it wasn't a hanging, and it wasn't the beginning of a war. It was a hot-air balloon launching, the first of its kind in the history of the United States.

The event had been highly publicized for the past several weeks in *Dunlap's American Daily Advertiser.* According to the paper, at exactly 10:00 A.M. on this glorious day, the famed French aeronaut, or balloonist, Jean Pierre Blanchard would attempt a hydrogen-filled gas balloon ascension, weather permitting. For a price of $5.00 each, patrons would be admitted inside the prison yard to witness his departure.

Blanchard was well known and everyone wanted to rub elbows with him. He had earned a place in history as the first man, along with an American doctor John Jeffries, to fly across the English Channel in a hot air balloon in 1785. Blanchard was a zestful and handsome scientist who loved inventing contraptions. At the age of twelve, he invented a rat trap that would shoot off a pistol and kill the trapped animal. As he got older he became fascinated with flying machines and, on March 2, 1784, made his first successful ascent in a balloon that he built himself. Since then he had made a total of forty-four hot-air balloon demonstrations to people all over Europe.

Once Blanchard had set his mind to this historical first in the United States, he just needed to pick a place, a date, and a time, which he recorded along with other details in his *Journal of My Forty-Fifth Ascension*. He chose Philadelphia because it was a major city. He chose the prison yard as his takeoff point for several reasons. First, his balloon and the hydrogen-making "ventilator" could be protected from vandals during his flight preparation—a funny thought since all the prisoners were inside the walls! Second, the walls of the prison would protect the balloon from damage from the brisk winter wind while he was inflating it. Third, if he had the event take place inside the prison, he could charge an admission fee! The prison yard could hold about 4,800 people. At $5.00 a head, there was a potential to make $24,000, which was not a bad sum back in 1793. Unfortunately, most people decided they didn't need to see the actual liftoff, so only one hundred spectators paid. The rest were satisfied to wait outside the yard for the balloon to pop its head over the prison walls and float into the sky. Blanchard made a total of $405 from the ticket sales, plus another $263 in donations from science enthusiasts, which was hardly enough to defray his $1,500 worth of expenses.

The drama began with a brass band playing as the famous Frenchman walked into the prison courtyard and bowed to the paying spectators and cheering crowd. His short, fit figure was dressed in style, sporting bright blue knee breeches with a matching waistcoat and a hat with white feathers. He looked like an actor ready to take the stage. The crowd outside heard the cheers and were anxious for it all to begin, while the paying crowd inside watched in amazement as Blanchard carefully set up the balloon. He laid out the varnished yellow silk balloon on the floor. Then he aimed the hydrogen-making ventilator and filled up the balloon. The people oohed and aahed as it grew larger and larger. He had several assistants holding the ropes that were attached to the balloon so that the balloon wouldn't take off until he was ready.

Meanwhile, a carriage with none other than the chief executive himself, President George Washington, pulled up to the prison gates. As he stepped down from the carriage, the crowd fell silent and bowed and nodded in respect. Fifteen cannons boomed, saluting the chief. With him were also the French ambassador and other notables. As the ensemble of dignitaries entered the yard, the crowd parted. Blanchard stood before his brightly inflated balloon at attention. As the president approached, Blanchard took off his feathered hat and bowed gracefully, thanking the distinguished guests for coming.

President Washington then handed Blanchard a "passport," which would assure Mr. Blanchard help wherever he and the balloon happened to land. It read,

> To All Whom these Presents Shall Come: The bearer hereof, Mr. Blanchard a citizen of France, proposing to ascend in a balloon from the city of Philadelphia at 10 o'clock, A.M. this day, to pass in such place as circumstances may render most convenient, these are therefore to recommend to all citizens of the United States, and others, that in his passage, descent, return or journeying elsewhere, they oppose no hindrance or molestation to the said Mr. Blanchard; and, that on the contrary, they receive and aid him with that humanity and good will which may render honour to their country, and justice to an individual so distinguished by his efforts to establish and advance in art, in order to make it useful to mankind in general.

It was signed, "George Washington."

Blanchard once again bowed and thanked him. He would carry this letter, the first "airmail" letter, with him for his landing. Now he excused himself and was ready to ascend. As he did, a well-wisher shoved a small black dog into Blanchard's arm and he reluctantly took it. He put the dog in the wicker basket, waved to the crowd, and then climbed in himself. Washington shook his hand and wished him bon voyage.

At exactly 9:10 the balloon rose easily out of the prison courtyard. The crowd was in awe. Blanchard saluted the crowd with a special flag he had made for the event, which had the armor bearings of the United States on one side and the colors of the French flag on the other. The balloon rose to "200 fathoms," or 1,200 feet, and was carried northwest towards the Delaware River. One dignitary, General John Steele, the comptroller of the U.S. Treasury, commented, "Seeing the man waving a flag at an immense height from the ground, was the most interesting sight that I ever beheld. . . . I could not help trembling for his safety."

Indeed, even though Blanchard had done this many times before, he saw the need for a backup plan and had tried to invent some kind of parachute, which had only been tested (successfully) on animals. In other words, if he accidentally fell out of the balloon, he would likely tumble to his death. Nonetheless, Blanchard was in high spirits as the balloon leveled off at around 5,800 feet over the glistening water of the Delaware River.

At this point, jotting notes in his journal, he decided to play the part of the dedicated scientist and started to do some experiments. He checked his pulse with a pocket watch and carefully noted that his pulse was "92 pulsations in the minute whereas on the ground I had experienced no more than 84 in the same given time." He then filled six bottles with "atmospherical air," which he did whenever he was floating. He sealed the bottles to examine the air later, "as the accuracy of the experiment required." He then weighed a stone that on the ground weighed 5½ ounces but at that altitude only weighed 4 ounces.

The wind was now carrying him over to the Jersey side, and Blanchard knew he should find a clear place to land before he hit the Atlantic Ocean. He picked a spot in an open field and carefully guided the balloon using the gas valves and ballast weights till the balloon was safely on the ground. He landed in a farm field in Woodbury, New Jersey. As soon as the balloon hit the ground, the dog jumped out of the basket and headed for the nearest tree to relieve himself. The entire flight was forty-six minutes and covered a distance of 15 miles.

The only problem now was how to get himself and his balloon safely back to Philadelphia, where an anxious crowd awaited the outcome of this historic flight. Blanchard took out a compass and tried to figure out exactly where he was. As he spun the compass around, he wound up facing a farmer who was staring at him in a stupor.

The farmer apparently had no clue about what had just transpired. All he knew was that some strange man and his dog just dropped out of the sky and landed on his farm. Blanchard, who was not very skilled at the English language, tried to explain in broken English what he was doing and that he needed help. He could see that he was not getting through to the farmer, so he held up a bottle of wine and motioned the farmer toward him. Blanchard took a swig first to show the man it wasn't poisoned. The farmer inched forward, took a swig himself, and smiled. Blanchard showed the man his "passport" but the farmer couldn't read. However, he did understand the name Washington.

While Blanchard was trying to explain to the farmer that he needed a ride back, a second farmer approached with a shotgun aimed at the balloon, which was now lying on its side. The downed balloon moved slightly in the wind, and the second farmer dropped to his knees and started to pray for this alien life force to go away. The first farmer calmed the kneeling man by telling him that Blanchard had some connection to President Washington and showed him the letter. Since the second farmer could read a bit, he was able to understand enough that they were supposed to help this man.

The two farmers gathered a bunch of their friends. Several of them helped Blanchard fold the balloon and then placed it in one of their wagons. The group then escorted Blanchard to Cooper's Ferry, which was on the bank of the Delaware River. Before he got on the boat, however, Blanchard pulled out a piece of paper and asked them to certify that he had landed the balloon in "Deptford Township, County of Gloucester in the State of New Jersey, about 10 0'clock 56 minutes, A.M. . . . on the ninth of January, anno Domini, 1793." The farmers happily obliged, not realizing that by doing so they too now had become a part of history. Blanchard tucked his paperwork away, waved goodbye to his newfound friends, and rode the ferry safely back to the Pennsylvania side of the river.

Jean Pierre Blanchard was greeted by a cheering crowd who stood in line for hours to shake his hand. By 7:00 that evening, when all the well-wishers were gone, Blanchard met with Washington and presented him with the flag that was attached to the balloon during the historic flight. Washington thanked him and acknowledged that the balloon flight had a deep effect on all who saw it.

Blanchard stayed in Philadelphia for a while. He was offered free office space and opened up an "aerostatical laboratory" where he kept his balloon and some mechanical inventions, like a mechanical eagle that flapped its own wings. He charged a 25-cent admission fee. He tried to raise money to do a second balloon flight but was not able to do so; however, he performed a couple of demonstrations sending dogs, cats, and squirrels up and having them descend by a makeshift parachute.

Eventually he went back to Europe and did thirteen more flights. In February 1808, Blanchard suffered a heart attack on a flight over the Netherlands and fell 50 feet to the ground. He never recovered from the fall and died on March 7, 1809.

Blanchard is known to the world as an innovator in flight and the first person to get public attention for manned flights.

His fifty-nine ascensions lead the way for other scientific achievements in space. He was daring, he was innovative, and he was the first: the first to fly a manned flight, the first to carry an airmail letter, and the first to do experiments in the air. And proudly, Pennsylvanians can say it happened in their state.

An Expedition
in Search of
a Beginning
· 1803 ·

At ten o'clock on a sultry summer morning, the Lewis and Clark expedition got off to a "rocky" start, literally and figuratively, from the city of Pittsburgh. This was not the day the journey was supposed to begin. This was not the starting point originally planned for this all-important mission. And the team that was packing to leave was missing a rather important member: Clark.

This was a vital mission by everyone's standards. No one in the United States knew for sure what lay beyond the plains west of the Mississippi. There was the possibility of great wealth to be found. Gold and silver, abundant furs, and most important of all, a passage by water to the great Pacific Ocean were high priorities for the struggling young nation. President Thomas Jefferson's plan for a "literary," meaning scientific, expedition of the vast western territories currently under Spanish rule was risky for a number of reasons. First, the United States didn't own the land. President Jefferson was planning an illegal mission to help secure and then defend the territory. On November 30, 1803, while Jefferson and others were in the early stages of planning the expedition, France gained control of the territory by bamboozling Spain. France promised not to sell the land to the United States—and yet just twenty days later did exactly that. France sold the land to the United States on December 20, 1803, despite its promise to Spain. Suddenly the mission took on a new meaning, since now the Americans could attempt to build positive relations with the Indian tribes while also scouting the terrain for military purposes. Adding this strategic element to the burden of simply traveling and charting these unknown lands made this operation an epic adventure.

With all this in mind, Meriwether Lewis went about following his orders. He was instructed to plan the expedition and learn everything necessary to make it a complete success. Extensive training in science, mapmaking, botany, medicine, and diplomacy were arranged, mostly in Philadelphia. The leading men in their fields were engaged to help Lewis. Throughout the entire year before the start of the journey, Lewis kept busy with the details. The starting point for the expedition was changed from Nashville, Tennessee, to Pittsburgh. Pittsburgh is much closer to Washington, D.C., and Philadelphia, and it would be much more convenient to ship supplies to western Pennsylvania than to Nashville. Furthermore, Pittsburgh was a logical starting point. The Ohio River is formed in Pittsburgh by the meeting of the Allegheny and Monongahela rivers. Since this was primarily to be a river trip, the travelers could ride right down the Ohio to the Mississippi then on to the Missouri River. Thus, Lewis contacted a boatbuilder in Pittsburgh to start work on a specially designed craft.

With the Louisiana Purchase becoming a reality, the bigwigs in Washington realized they had better have a backup leader for Meriwether Lewis. This vast new addition to the United States would require the expedition to consider how the territory might best be defended. Someone with more military and Indian experience would improve the chances for success. This prompted Lewis to write his good friend and former army cohort William Clark to join him on this adventure as coleader.

Clark was assured in the letter that he would be reinstated in the Army at the advanced rank of captain, the same rank Lewis held, to avoid any uncomfortable feelings between the two men and their followers. This was very important to Lewis, as when they had last parted Clark was his superior.

Everything was coming together. Lewis left the White House and started off for Pittsburgh. Supplies were being hauled over land so that once Lewis arrived in Pittsburgh, he would be able to load his new boat and begin his lengthy trek. Despite Lewis's best intentions, everything began slipping behind schedule. Lewis was hoping to make winter camp well up the Missouri River. That goal put Captain Lewis in a hurried state. He arrived in Pittsburgh on July 15, and as soon as he arranged accommodations, he went off to see his new boat. All his planning, work, and worry were about to go seriously awry, for the boat was not ready. There are no known records of the boatbuilder's name, but what is known is that the builder met Captain Meriwether Lewis drunk and full of bluster. He complained of problems with his workers and trouble finding materials, but the bottom line was the boat was nowhere near ready to go.

In utter disgust and frustration, Lewis went about looking for another craftsman. Such was the shortage of boatbuilding professionals at the time that he could only return to his original builder and cajole, berate, and browbeat the man into a more productive state. Lewis returned to the boatyard day after day. Progress was slow. The builder's fondness for drink and the continued labor problems were aggravated by the lack of building materials.

Lewis considered all his options. One thought was to buy a number of smaller vessels called pirogues. These were large dugout canoes of an Indian design. His hope was that he could start out with these and have a builder downriver get to work on a new boat. Everyone in Pittsburgh assured him that this would be futile. There were no builders anywhere downriver who could be counted on to perform this vital job.

The real problem was that the expedition required a specially designed boat. It needed to carry an incredible amount of supplies, and sturdy construction was essential. It would have to hold up under brutal conditions. The solid keel running from front to back would need to withstand rocks and sandbars in low water. It would have to carry a massive load of provisions through shallow waters, and it would need to be light enough to pull or push when the water was too low. Without a doubt, a master boatbuilder was required; unfortunately, the only one available was a drunk.

Days were turning into weeks. A further complication was making matters worse by the hour: The summer of 1803 was one of the driest in memory. Drought conditions were causing the Ohio River to get lower and lower. The dwindling water meant that the venture downriver would be slow and laborious. The President's missives to get underway were demoralizing as Lewis could do nothing more than show up at the boat-yard and prod the workers to hurry.

One good piece of news arrived by mail. A letter from William Clark finally caught up to Lewis in Pittsburgh. It had taken a circuitous route around the eastern seaboard. Clark's reply was that he was honored and pleased to accompany his old friend on this arduous but possibly glorious, adventure. His exact words were: "I do assure you no man lives with whom I would prefur [sic] to undertake such a trip as yourself."

Clark was living in southern Indiana at the time and would be able to meet Lewis on the Ohio River. He was also procuring able-bodied men to help on the trip. Clark was especially looking for strong men, knowing the boat would be loaded and unloaded many times. Clark and Lewis agreed that single men would be preferable. They would also have to belong to the military or be willing to join. Manning the expedition would become an ongoing problem throughout the trip—that is, if Lewis could even get his boat built and get started.

Supplies had arrived from different locations. The latest army-issue rifles were stored and ready to go. Medicines, books, tarps, sails, and foodstuffs sat at the ready. A large quantity of a specially made soup that was boiled down from beef into a thick paste and then stored in sealed lead canisters arrived from Philadelphia. Storing soup in something so heavy as lead seems self-defeating, but it made perfect sense and showed the true genius of the planning for this venture: As the soup was consumed, the canisters could be melted down to make bullets.

At 7:00 A.M. on August 31, the boat was pronounced ready to go. Lewis supervised the loading of the vessel. In a mere three hours the daring passage was ready to begin. At 10:00 A.M. sharp, with the boat fully loaded and an extra pirogue packed to lessen the weight, the most important expedition in U.S. history began.

The Ohio River meanders out of Pennsylvania, and the low water levels required that a great deal of the provisions be sent by wagon to Wheeling, in what is now West Virginia, to be picked up en route. This was a wise decision because the depleted river was a nightmare to navigate. There were numerous times just in the first few days that the boat had to be completely emptied and dragged, sometimes with the help of a local farmer's livestock, through the shallow, rocky river.

Despite all the last-minute pitfalls and trials, Meriwether Lewis clawed and fought his way out of every bad situation. Eventually the Lewis and Clark expedition set out from Pittsburgh, Pennsylvania, and was an overwhelming success.

The Eastern State Penitentiary:
A Nice Place to Visit, but You Wouldn't Want to Live There
• 1829 •

As Charles Williams was "escorted" to the brand-new Eastern State Penitentiary, located on an old cherry orchard just outside of Philadelphia, he was a mere eighteen years of age. Although the weather on October 23, 1829, was not recorded in the annals of time, it is safe to say he would not have noticed either way. The building was tall, foreboding, and oozed gloom. It was built to look just that way and has been described as an ominous fortress. Even though it was still under construction, it was easy to spot the massive iron gates and the towering concrete castlelike towers. It is not hard to imagine just how imposing this structure and its purpose would be to its very first inmate.

This new prison was an idea hatched by Quakers such as Dr. Benjamin Rush and the seemingly omnipresent Benjamin Franklin. They were members of a group that fought for major prison reform. They wrote that the outward appearance should be "a cheerless blank indicative of the misery which awaits the unhappy being who enters." Not that prisons of the day were cheerful or lacking in misery; on the contrary, in those days prisons were foul, diseased cesspools. Inmates could expect cruel treatment and beatings as the accepted norm.

Perhaps Charles Williams reconsidered his crimes briefly when the new warden greeted him in person once he had passed through three different sets of daunting doors and was well inside the building. Mr. Williams was a burglar. His prison record shows that he stole a $20.00 watch, a $3.00 gold seal, and a gold key. He had been sentenced to two years of imprisonment for these crimes. His prison documents also tell us he was a farmer by trade and that he could read.

Once inside, Charles immediately had something taken from him: his name. Number 1 was his new name, as he was the first prisoner to grace these walls, and for the rest of his stay, that was the only way that anyone would refer to him. Next, Number 1 had his clothing stripped off; he was measured, weighed, and given a physical examination. All of his pertinent information was recorded for posterity. His complexion, hair and eye color, age, and the length of his feet were all dutifully marked down in his file. One can only wonder as to the relevance of his foot size, but there it was for any prison staff member to look up.

He was then dressed in the official uniform of the establishment. Wool pants, a jacket with his new numerical identity sewn on the front, two handkerchiefs, two pairs of socks, and a pair of shoes made up the entire ensemble. Obviously fashion was not a big concern.

He must have been surprised at the next action. They put a black sack over his head and led him to his own private cell. The belief at the time was that, should the prisoner get free within the building, he would be disoriented from never having seen his way around. When he arrived at his cell, the sack was removed, and for the next two years, the guard was the only person he ever saw. His guard explained the rules: There was to be no talking, or for that matter no communication, with anyone. The only person he could speak with was a prison official and then only when asked to respond. His meals would be served to him alone in his cell. He could have no books or papers. The only exception to this rule was the Bible. This was a Quaker facility, after all. There would be no singing, no whistling, nor any type of game or diversion. The prisoner known only as Number 1 was to spend his time in a state of penance; that is, to be penitent. Thus was born a new meaning for the word *penitentiary*.

There was one positive aspect of prison life for Charles. He was permitted to spend one hour each day in the recreation yard. He would still be alone, but he could walk back and forth in the great outdoors. Never mind that the great outdoors was surrounded by walls that were 30 feet high and 12 feet thick at the base. On his way to the recreation yard and back, his guard would accompany him. The black hood was in place through the halls so he could see no other inmates and they could not see him.

Other than this brief respite, his day was only interrupted by meals. He sat in his cell with nothing to do. He had no work; he had no play. The Quakers knew the results this would achieve: "His mind can only operate on itself; generally, but a few hours elapse before he petitions for something to do, and for a Bible. No instance has occurred, in which such a petition has been delayed beyond a day or two."

With no other source of diversion, it could be assumed that the inmates used the Bible to teach themselves everything from how to read to the Scriptures themselves. Two things would be a sure bet for any of these early inmates. First, they most probably felt true regret for their crimes and, second, their Bibles were very well read.

Of course a lot was going on outside of the prisoner's view. Had Charles been able to take a look around the prison, he would have seen one of the true construction marvels of its time. The penitentiary was reputed to be the most expensive building in North America, built at a cost of $772,600. Each of the seven original cellblocks radiated out from a central rotunda. This design allowed for one set of guards to monitor every hall simultaneously and won its young architect, John Haviland, a $100 prize. His blueprint included solitary confinement cells for 250 prisoners. Each cell had running water and a toilet, an unheard-of luxury in 1829. Unfortunately for the convicts, the sewage system did not work well, and the stench must have added to the penalty they already endured. Each of the rooms was small and windowless, although they each had a skylight, presumably to better communicate with God.

This new penitentiary, designed and run by Quakers, was meant to show their strictness as well as their benevolence. There were to be no beatings or lashings at this institution. While these barbaric methods were the stock-in-trade of prisons that came before, the Quakers believed that solitude and penance would be enough to reform a man. Originally the only extra punishment was to have a meal withheld. Any type of talking or communicating, even talking to oneself, was reason enough to cause an inmate to miss a meal or two.

Human nature being what it is, these paltry punishments did little to dissuade the captives from misbehaving. It wasn't long before some innovative retributions that the Quakers never would have approved of became commonplace. The straightjacket, the water bath, the mad chair, and the ghastly iron gag all became tools for the jailers to subdue the incorrigibles.

Suffice it to say, all of these torturous methods were used without Quaker approval; however, guards or prison officials possessing some sadistic tendencies were known to apply them.

Despite some of these unsavory occurrences, the Eastern State Penitentiary, or Cherry Hill as it was popularly called, was a model for prison reform. More than 300 prisons were constructed worldwide based on its hub-and-spoke design. From its very inception it was a tourist attraction, drawing more than 10,000 visitors a year by midcentury. The Quakers had led the way for the concept of prison reform, in spite of the fact that detractors thought the isolation of solitary confinement was in itself cruel and unusual punishment. These critics claimed that the system produced a high rate of mental illness. This has not been documented, but it may be a fair assessment.

As the years rolled by, the prison reformed itself again and again. Many of the early tortures were discontinued. The prison housed many famous and infamous criminals through the years. Probably the most famous inmate was Alphonse "Scar-face" Capone. The mobster from Chicago spent the better part of a year as a "guest" at Eastern State after being picked up on a concealed weapons charge shortly after the Saint Valentine's Day Massacre. In 1929, the August 20 edition of the *Philadelphia Public Ledger* described Al's cell: "The whole room was suffused in the glow of a desk lamp which stood on a polished desk. . . . On the once grim walls of the penal chamber hung tasteful paintings, and the strains of a waltz were being emitted by a powerful cabinet radio receiver of handsome design and fine finish." Of course Capone's was the only "fixed up" cell in the entire prison. Apparently his power and connections reached all the way from Chicago to Philadelphia.

It is interesting to compare the description of Capone's accommodations to this early quote by Dr. Benjamin Rush. In 1787 he wrote this rendition of his concept of the new reform prison: "Let the avenue to this house be rendered difficult and gloomy by mountains and morasses. Let the doors be of iron, and let the grating, occasioned by opening and shutting them, be increased by an echo that shall deeply pierce the soul."

The Eastern State Penitentiary remained functional as a prison for 142 years until it closed in 1971. That's 140 years after Charles Williams traded his Number 1 to get his name back and rejoin society. Who is to say if he was reformed, but it seems a safe bet that he quoted Biblical scriptures.

The Lost Children of the Alleghenies
·1856·

Some years, winter in the Allegheny Mountains of western Pennsylvania holds on a little longer than in other years. Such was the case in late April of the winter of 1856, when patches of snow were scattered around like bedsheets blown off of clotheslines.

A young family, typical settlers of the time, had put down stakes in a small log cabin located just outside the town of Lovely, Pennsylvania. Although most people would have trouble finding it on a map, the community was called Spruce Hollow. The family included Samuel Cox, his wife, Susannah, and their two young boys, seven-year-old George and five-year-old Joseph.

Samuel supported his family in a typical way for the times. They had a good vegetable garden, plus Samuel's hunting skills to provide meat for the table. Unfortunately, their quiet rural lifestyle was about to become a nightmare.

Early on the morning of April 25, 1856, as the family was enjoying breakfast, the family dog started a commotion outside. Typically this meant that an animal had wondered into the area, and anyone who lives by wild game was naturally quick to investigate. Samuel did just that, grabbing his rifle and heading out after his barking hunting dog.

He pursued the dog deep into the woods with no luck. Since he was already out, he decided to roam around to see if he could scare up something for Susannah's dinner table. Meanwhile, George and Joseph decided to find their dad. They might have been hoping for one of the great prizes that could result from their father's hunting endeavors, like a lucky rabbit's foot or maybe the tail of a raccoon. Their mother probably didn't worry when they wandered off, since they had been out with their dad many times before.

By the time Samuel wandered back home from his excursion, the boys had been out in the woods quite a while. When Susannah realized the boys were not with their father, panic began to set in. She and Samuel rushed back into the woods to begin a frantic search.

The frontier forest of those times was no place for lost children. A wide variety of wild animals, including bears, wolves, and snakes, called that stretch of woods home. Streams and creeks were at their zeniths, so thoughts of drowning crept into Samuel's and Susannah's minds. It didn't take long before these frightened parents realized that they were going to need help to locate the boys before nightfall. Predators and high water were bad enough, but cold and hunger became additional concerns.

Samuel went about gathering neighbors and friends. In a time of crisis such as this, everyone pitched in. The word spread and soon there were many volunteers scouring the mountainsides and valleys, but with no luck. The night was cold, and Samuel and Susannah assumed the boys were only wearing light jackets. A very gloomy group of searchers quit for the night, with the promise of an early start and more reinforcements to come the next morning.

The next day dawned with even more frost and cold in the air. By now the word had spread and people came from miles around. Men were searching in their winter coats, and the first thoughts of failure began to seep into the minds of the rescue team as they wondered if the boys could have survived the frigid night. They plodded along, looking in the most obvious places. With the streams as high as they were, it was assumed that the boys would not ford the freezing waters. The search grid grew wider and wider.

The third day brought serious doubts. Had the boys been eaten by wild animals? Were they victims of the fast, high waters? Could they survive the elements? One day turned into another, but no one was willing to give up. What if those were their children? What if the boys were alive and clinging to the hope that someone would find them?

At the end of the first week, a woman claimed she heard the cries of a small child. Searchers rallied, to no avail. There was simply no sign of the boys anywhere. The volunteers had to make some very hard decisions. Many had farms that needed tending. It was the time of year for spring planting. People had their own families to consider. These were hard times. Still, they gathered every morning. *Put yourself in Samuel's place,* they thought. *What if those were your children out there?*

Eight days passed, and Samuel and Susannah were beside themselves, their worst fears always present in their minds. A meeting was held in the Bedford County courthouse, and a reward in the amount of $50 was collected. This brought even more people into the fold of searchers. Yet time slipped by with no clues at all.

Fifteen miles away, Jacob Dibert had heard of the tragedy that befell George and Joseph Cox. Living as he did on the other side of Blue Knob Mountain, it was impractical to leave his farm to help. Still, the missing boys preyed on his mind. As the days passed and his plowing and planting were caught up, he and his wife discussed the Cox's plight at length.

Word on the mountainside was that Jacob had dreams that occasionally came true, and he even confided in his wife that he wished that he could dream up where those little boys were. The very next day Jacob described a dream of a forest in a valley. He was not familiar with the forest, but the more he described it, the more it seemed like the forest of his wife's childhood. Her apparent familiarity with the area he described was of great interest as she came from a farm not that far from the Cox homestead.

Jacob dreamed that he was out searching for the boys. In the dream he came upon a dead deer and a little ways farther he found a boy's shoe. He proceeded to cross a stream, scrambling over a fallen log as a bridge. After following the stream a short ways, he came to an old tree, and there, curled up in the overgrown roots, were the bodies of the boys.

Jacob Dibert and his wife decided this was too much to ignore. Mrs. Dibert suggested that he head over to her father's home and enlist him in the search since he would have an even greater knowledge of the local terrain. Jacob set out to do just that but found the older man to be away from the family farm. The only one there was Jacob's brother-in-law, Harrison Whysong. Harrison patiently listened to the dream story and conveyed his feelings that it was just so much foolishness. Still, he saw no point in Jacob wandering out in the woods alone with no hope of finding the landmarks that he himself did in fact recognize. He agreed to accompany Jacob along his dream path.

Maybe he lost some of his doubt when they came across a dead deer exactly as Jacob had described. Soon after that a boy's shoe lay directly in their path. Before long they were racing across the log bridge over the stream. Just a bit farther they saw the old tree with its gnarled roots cradling the bodies of the Cox boys, just as Jacob had dreamed it.

Joseph was said to be huddled in his older brother's arms, his head resting on a makeshift pillow of his brother's hat. It was estimated that the boys had died about four days earlier. They had been lost for two weeks.

Samuel Cox was brought to the site to retrieve his sons. After the funeral the boys were laid to rest in a single grave with a single headstone. Jacob Dibert and Harrison Whysong gave up their reward money to purchase the tombstone. A monument was placed in 1906 near the small town of Pavia at the spot where the boys were found.

Samuel and Susannah Cox had seven more children, of whom only four survived childhood. One of those children was Sam Cox, the great-great-uncle of Scott Bruce, coauthor of this book.

The tale of the "Lost Children" grew, becoming a story used in the primer books of schoolchildren in the area. This story was used to help children learn to read, write, and spell. The author's father was familiar with this story from his grade school book, without knowing that the boys were his great-uncles.

The forests around Blue Knob Mountain are still pretty wild. Very little has changed. If you go for a visit, it is easy to imagine the throngs of concerned neighbors wandering the trails and calling out for the boys, for in this area, time has stood still. It is a place where neighbors still help neighbors.

Well . . . That's a Deep Subject
·1859·

Every man, woman, and child today is familiar with the term "oil well." Oil wells are a part of our everyday life. Naturally, this was not true back in August of 1859. In fact, until "Colonel" Edwin Drake came to northwest Pennsylvania, there was no such thing as an oil well. For that matter, there was no such person as "Colonel" Edwin Drake, either. The man was never "Colonel" of anything: Mr. Drake and his financial backers invented the title to impress the locals. But we are getting ahead of ourselves. Let's back up a little to see how this story unfolds.

Long before Edwin Drake was born, even before Columbus sailed from Spain, oil leaked from the rocks and ground of western Pennsylvania. Early Native Americans may have collected oil from these "seeps" to use for medicinal purposes. The first European settlers harvested this oil for use as fuel in lamps and lanterns as well as a lubricant for the crude machines of the day.

By the 1850s people were looking into future possibilities for the strange oil that leaked out of the ground. One such person was George Bissel, a New York lawyer. His plan was to produce oil for a variety of commercial purposes. To that end, he hired one of America's leading chemists, Benjamin Silliman Jr., to determine if this "crude oil" that he brought back from western Pennsylvania to New York could be used in a manner similar to other petroleum products. The hope was that it could be distilled into an illuminant for lamps and lanterns. Silliman made great progress in this area and eventually found that the crude oil could be distilled into several different products; one of these was a very high-quality lamp fuel. This was very exciting technology in these days before the coming of commercial electricity. Bissell was convinced that there was a very large market for this oil.

Armed with the information he needed, Bissell went about creating the financial backing to proceed with his business plan. His primary funder was James Townsend, the president of a bank in New Haven, Connecticut. Together with others they formed the Pennsylvania Rock Oil Company.

With a plan and funding in hand, it was time for action. The first step was to find someone to go to Titusville, Pennsylvania, which was known to be an oil-rich area. Staying at the same hotel in New Haven where Bissell had met with Townsend was a man looking for a job. Edwin L. Drake had no special talents or abilities in the oil, engineering, or surveying fields. What he did have was a free railroad ticket left over from his days working for the railroad, and this was enough to get him hired. Having a free railroad ticket as one's primary job qualification provides an early hint as to the shoestring budget of this whole operation. It was during this expedition that Townsend, through his communications with Drake, created the tongue-in-cheek moniker "Colonel" Drake.

Drake first visited Titusville in December of 1857. His employers, having changed their name from the Pennsylvania Rock Oil Company to the Seneca Oil Company, assigned him a number of tasks including some title work and a report on the seep.

Drake returned to Titusville the following year, but now he had an official position as the general agent of the company, in charge of operations. He was also a minor stockholder. He began immediately to improve on an existing oil collection site.

This effort was his first of many failures. When he arrived, the maximum amount of oil collected daily was a paltry three or four gallons. Drake managed to improve that to about ten gallons a day, but certainly not the vast quantities needed to make this operation a success. He hired men to open up other springs, and when that didn't net him positive results, he made his first attempts at digging a shaft. All of these attempts failed as well. The shafts soon filled with water, making the work hopeless.

These obviously failed methods led Drake to try something completely different. He decided to drill a well using the current methods of the salt drillers. Salt drillers had been drilling wells prior to this time and hitting oil. The problem was they were not looking for oil. They were looking for salt water. Drake's was the first salt well drilled for the purpose of finding crude oil. This new concept struck the locals as a mild form of madness. The idea of "drilling" for oil was laughable in their eyes. Soon Edwin had quite a few detractors, who referred to the whole process as Drake's Folly.

Drake's driller, a salt driller by the name of William "Uncle Billy" Smith, was getting close to despair. Every hole kept caving. Aside from his tenacity, Drake made a huge contribution during this attempt. He came up with the concept of a drive pipe, which consisted of 10-foot lengths of pipe made from sturdy cast iron. Drake and Uncle Billy literally beat the pipe into the ground all the way down to the bedrock. The drilling tools could be lowered through the pipe and the effects of caving were neutralized. Now Uncle Billy could effectively drill through the bedrock. Because it was mostly shale, it too occasionally caved, but progress was being made at the rate of almost 3 feet a day.

New problems arose on a daily basis. Then came the biggest blow of all: The company funds dried up. Drake had been managing on a meager budget, but now there was no more money. Nonetheless, this very determined man was not going to let anything stop him. He started using his own money, and in no time that resource was depleted too. He resorted to borrowing money. Two friends signed a note at a local bank so Drake could pour another $500 into his personal pit of despair.

On Saturday, August 27, 1859, at a depth of 69 feet, fortune smiled on Edwin Drake. Though he went home that Saturday night with no illusions that he was close to success, some magic was working below the surface of the well site.

The next morning, Uncle Billy and his young son Samuel arrived at the well site. Oil was bubbling up through the hole. There do not seem to be reliable accounts of exactly how much crude oil was collected from this first successful well, but the smallest estimates have it at about ten barrels a day. Compared to the ten gallons a day from Drake's start, this was an absolute winner. A simple hand-operated water pump pulled this volume from the ground. The more important result was that Drake's new method of "drilling" for oil was a complete success. Soon the entire area was filled to capacity with oil wells.

Drake never patented the system he invented utilizing the drive pipe. That alone would have assured him a very rosy future. He drilled other wells in the area but never ventured out on his own. Drake had no further fame in his lifetime and eventually died penniless.

With Drake's help, Pennsylvania led the world in oil production, producing 50 percent of the entire world's output until the Texas oil boom of 1901. Not much oil is pulled out of the ground in Pennsylvania anymore, but that small amount is considered to be of the highest quality.

Edwin Drake is honored today at the Drake Well Museum in northwestern Pennsylvania. Despite his numerous failures, he fathered an entire industry and started the rush to find Black Gold!

The Battle of Gettysburg: (It Wasn't about Shoes After All.)

· 1863 ·

A tiny little town in south-central Pennsylvania played an unlikely host to the biggest battle ever staged on American soil. This single three-day clash was responsible for over 50,000 casualties and was the turning point in the Civil War.

Gettysburg, Pennsylvania, marked the northern-most point on the map infiltrated by Confederate General Robert E. Lee and his grand Army of Northern Virginia. Fresh off a major victory at the Battle of Chancellorsville in early May, Lee brought his company of 75,000 men into Pennsylvania to menace the state capital at Harrisburg, just north of Gettysburg. He also needed supplies for his soldiers, such as food, dry goods, and shoes, and they were much more bountiful in the North where the fighting had yet to devastate the land.

The Confederate army marched north from the Shenandoah Valley in Virginia, roughly following what is now Interstate 81, until they were positioned in an arc to the west and north of Gettysburg.

Meanwhile, to the east and south were the protectors of the northern cities of Baltimore and Washington, D.C. The Federal Army of the Potomac was stringing itself out as a barrier to keep the "rebs" from storming into these strongholds and wreaking havoc. The Army of the Potomac was experiencing a crucial change in leadership at this time. President Abraham Lincoln had just accepted the resignation of the very colorful General Joseph Hooker. His replacement, Major General George Gordon Meade, was put in charge of 90,000 troops with the sole purpose of stopping Lee's advance.

The Battle of Gettysburg was not a planned battle. None of the generals had looked at a map and decided this would be a good location for a confrontation. A more likely scenario is that Lee was aiming for Harrisburg or possibly even Philadelphia for his next major confrontation. He had instructed his generals and subordinates not to engage the enemy until he could do so at full strength. Once General Lee received word that the Federal army had crossed the Potomac in pursuit of him, he ordered his troops to tighten up, readying for a fight. His main encampment was to be in a small community called Cashtown, located about 8 miles west of Gettysburg. This was chosen as a central location to gather his forces, which had spread from Carlisle in the south to Harrisburg in the north. At the time there was only a small contingent of Federals camped in Gettysburg.

One of the Confederate brigades undertook a mission into Gettysburg in search of supplies, including shoes. This foray is the source of a legend that lives on today, which tells that the Battle of Gettysburg was fought because shoe-hunting rebels stumbled into unsuspecting Yankees. In fact there was no reason to believe that Confederate forces thought there might be some large cache of shoes in Gettysburg. There were no shoe factories there, nor was there any indication that any supplies might be available in quantity. The Confederate brigade, led by

J. Johnston Pettigrew, wisely returned to Cashtown upon noticing the Federal troops camped there.

Pettigrew's report precipitated the first big mistake on the part of the Southerners. When Pettigrew reported finding a small enemy force to General Henry Heth, his division commander, Heth decided to send some troops back looking for a fight, not footwear. It is believed that Heth later claimed to have heard of a stockpile of shoes to cover the fact that he had sent troops into battle before Lee could properly gather his regiments.

John Buford was in charge of the Union army camped in Gettysburg. In truth Buford was outnumbered, but his men were better armed than the Confederates because they were outfitted with the new Spencer repeating rifles, lending a distinct advantage in firepower. Buford's troops held against the attacking soldiers in the skirmish until help arrived in the form of the Federal First Corps, sweeping up from the south. The reinforcements provided the necessary military capability to overwhelm the invaders and take several hundred captives. The Battle of Gettysburg had begun. Now it was a race for the two sides to gather their respective armies for a serious challenge.

The rest of the day saw fighting everywhere. Ironically, Union troops stormed in from the south and east, while Confederate soldiers poured down from the north and west. The Southerners had the advantage in numbers with 25,000 troops flooding in against 18,000 Union regulars. However, the Northerners had the advantage of occupying the strongest locations. Vantage points like Cemetery Hill and Little Round Top were more easily defended. Perhaps one of the most ironic things about this battlefield was the sign on the cemetery gate from which Cemetery Hill took its name. The sign read, ALL PERSONS FOUND USING FIREARMS IN THESE GROUNDS WILL BE PROSECUTED WITH THE UTMOST RIGOR OF THE LAW. Day One of the fighting ranks in the top twenty-five largest battles of the war.

As the first day of fighting came to a close, the Confederate army had gained the most ground. Nonetheless, General Lee was disappointed that some of his commanders did not press the fight when they had opportunities: He knew that small mistakes had cost the South precious advantages. Still, the rebel army could count the day as victorious. As for the Federals, General Meade only arrived at the battlefield near midnight and immediately inspected the Union lines. The battleground was set for a chess match that was all too real.

The second day of this great battle dawned with more hope for the Union. In addition to holding the more defensible ground, they also saw their reinforcements building faster than their opponents'. Both leaders were trying to get a lay of the land in an effort to gain any edge in combat. General Lee's plan involved hitting the center of the Union line in a constant, unrelenting attack.

Most of this day's fighting took place in locations with evocative names such as Peach Orchard, Devil's Den, Wheat Field, and The Valley of Death. Nevertheless, these interesting names could not mask the carnage of the day. Deadly fighting and masterful maneuvering continued well into the night, producing nothing more than a stalemate punctuated with bloodshed.

Friday, July 3, began with Lee using the same basic plan of pummeling the middle ground of the battlefield in hopes of creating a breach. When that met with only limited success, the great Southern general was forced to change his tactics. With temperatures soaring to an unbearable 87 degrees F, both Yank and Reb alike suffered as Lee gathered his artillery for a barrage that was the most deafening noise ever heard. One hundred and forty-two Confederate cannons spewed forth a barrage on the Union army. After about fifteen minutes, the Union responded in kind with eighty or more cannons of their own. Accounts differ on the length of this bombardment, but most agree that it dragged on for well over an hour. The cannons were silenced for two reasons. First, the Confederate Army was running very low on artillery munitions. Second, the blasting did not have the desired effect. Union forces were not moved by a significant margin.

When the cannons stopped booming, nearly 13,000 Confederate men made their dash advancing over half a mile of open field in a desperate attempt to break the Union line. This attack was famously known as Pickett's Charge. In point of fact Pickett and his men only made up about one-third of the attack. The other two-thirds were comprised of supporting brigades led by General Trimble and General Pettigrew. Although the aggressors temporarily breached the opposing line, reinforcements rushed in and subdued the threat. Almost half the original 13,000 soldiers never made it back to their own side of the fight.

The fighting petered out, and the following day, July 4, was spent with the two fatigued armies staring at each other over the blood-soaked fields. General Robert E. Lee had met his match in General George G. Meade. It was time to give up the futile fight. The Confederate Army of Northern Virginia pulled out of Gettysburg the following day, with Meade giving only half-hearted pursuit. President Lincoln was distressed that Meade did not push harder to catch Lee and finish him off.

The town of Gettysburg was quiet but faced a cleanup of gigantic proportions. President Lincoln came to town four months later to dedicate the Soldiers' National Cemetery and deliver the now famous Gettysburg Address. There can be no better words to finish this chapter.

The Gettysburg Address

Four score and seven years ago our fathers brought forth on this continent a new nation, conceived in liberty and dedicated to the proposition that all men are created equal.

Now we are engaged in a great civil war, testing whether that nation or any nation so conceived and so dedicated can long endure. We are met on a great battlefield of that war. We have come to dedicate a portion of that field as a final resting-place for those who here gave their lives that that nation might live. It is altogether fitting and proper that we should do this.

But in a larger sense, we cannot dedicate, we cannot consecrate, we cannot hallow this ground. The brave men, living and dead who struggled here have consecrated it far above our poor power to add or detract. The world will little note nor long remember what we say here, but it can never forget what they did here. It is for us the living rather to be dedicated here to the unfinished work which they who fought here have thus far so nobly advanced. It is rather for us to be here dedicated to the great task remaining before us—that from these honored dead we take increased devotion to that cause for which they gave the last full measure of devotion—that we here highly resolve that these dead shall not have died in vain, that this nation under God shall have a new birth of freedom, and that government of the people, by the people, for the people shall not perish from the earth.

Abraham Lincoln
November 19, 1863

Memorial Day in Boalsburg
· 1864-1865 ·

Waterloo, New York, is customarily credited as being the very first place where Memorial Day was celebrated. However, there is conflicting information about when and where this holiday actually began. Sources reveal that the first celebration of Memorial Day did not take place in Waterloo but rather in the tiny town of Boalsburg right smack in the heart of Pennsylvania. The proof is irrefutable, but the arguments have gone on for a long time. The following explanation is not designed to pour fuel on the fire of those arguments. On the contrary, it is offered to recognize that many different communities all around the country came up with the same idea at nearly the same time. Furthermore, the whole idea of honoring our fallen heroes is such a wonderful concept that it would be disrespectful to hide its true origins.

It was a beautiful, clear fall day in central Pennsylvania in October of 1864. A teenage girl named Emma Hunter decided to go to the quaint little cemetery in Boalsburg to pay her respects to her father, the late Dr. Rueben Hunter. Dr. Hunter had been a dedicated physician who spent countless hours in the struggle of the Civil War trying to ease the pain of soldiers either wounded or diseased. Sadly, he contracted yellow fever from one of his warrior patients and became another casualty of war. Sophie Keller, a close friend, accompanied Emma on her visit to her father's grave. They gathered wildflowers and ferns along their walk to decorate the doctor's final resting place.

As they arrived at the cemetery, they happened upon an older woman named Elizabeth Meyer. She had chosen this same fine day to remember her son Amos. Amos had been a private in the Civil War and had the misfortune of losing his life on the last day of the Battle of Gettysburg at the tender age of nineteen. Elizabeth, like Emma and Sophie, had also come bearing flowers.

The two separate graves were in close proximity. The women got to talking and sharing stories about their loved ones. Emma spoke lovingly of her departed father and mentioned his profession and how he died trying to save lives. Elizabeth countered with the story of her son. She told how Amos had dropped his farming duties to enlist with the Union army near the very beginning of the war. She regaled the younger girls with stories of her son's bravery in various battles.

In a touching moment, Emma took some of her flowers and arranged them on the grave of Amos, which prompted Elizabeth to put some of her own cuttings on the plot of Dr. Hunter. The bond created by these women as they honored their departed family members gave such a feeling of satisfaction that it no doubt lessened the sad burden they held in common. The peaceful little cemetery that lay in the shadow of the majestic Mount Nittany was about to give birth to an important new holiday.

Up to this point in the tale, this chance meeting and exchange could not have been considered the beginning of what became Decoration Day and later Memorial Day. For time immemorial, all over this country and indeed all over the world, people have gone to burial grounds to honor the departed in this fashion. What makes this particular visit special is what the women did next.

Before they left the tended grounds of the cemetery, they made a pact to return the next year. The plan was to bring perhaps a few more friends and not only decorate their own loved ones' graves but to also decorate the graves of other soldiers who might not have anyone to look after them. Even at this point one might not consider this a momentous event. However, over the course of time as weeks turned to months, the women spoke of their compassionate mission with neighbors, friends, and acquaintances. The idea received an enthusiastic response throughout the small community. A date was agreed upon by the community to help foster the patriotic ideals, and the date they chose was July 4, 1865.

When the day finally arrived, what had been planned as a casual gathering by the two women had blossomed into a full-blown community ceremony. The entire town of Boalsburg, along with folks from neighboring communities, converged on the small cemetery.

Dr. George Hall, a local clergyman, preached an eloquent sermon. But there was more to this gathering than just piety. It was more like a wake, a celebration of fallen heroes and loved ones. In an impressive display of energy, the entire graveyard was decorated from end to end with flowers and American flags. Every single grave was dressed up for the party. That is what it was, a party. It was a celebration of the soldiers' lives and everyone who had participated in the making of this great, free nation.

The holiday was an immediate success. Each year the town gathered without fail, and to the present day it still does. Surrounding communities picked up on the event and started their own celebrations. Villages and cities across the country, unaware of Boalsburg's event, were creating similar gatherings to honor veterans as well.

Just four years after Emily and Elizabeth met in Boalsburg, an official order was issued, independent of any specific celebration, by General John A. Logan, commander in chief of the Grand Army of the Republic, designating May 30, 1868, as a day for ". . . decorating the graves of comrades who died in defense of their country." His hope was that it would be kept up from year to year, and of course this has come to pass. In 1882 the GAR (Grand Army of the Republic) advocated the "proper designation of May 30 as Memorial Day," not Decoration Day.

Many towns, villages, and communities lay claim as the birthplace of either Decoration Day or Memorial Day. A total of twenty-four separate locations believe theirs to have been the first, and it is easy to see why these beliefs are held. So many people felt the need to revere their lost loved ones that the practice popped up everywhere.

Interestingly, many of the original events only celebrated soldiers who fought for the Union Army. Southern communities created their own versions dedicated to their own heroes. The measures taken by the GAR were part of the government's efforts to bring the country back together after the divisive Civil War.

President Lyndon Johnson supposedly laid the controversy to rest. During his term of office in May of 1966, Johnson officially designated Waterloo, New York, as the birthplace of Memorial Day. His reasoning was sound and politically astute: That year would mark the one hundredth anniversary of Waterloo's event. Waterloo's first celebration was also a very well-planned and coordinated event. There was a band playing martial music in addition to the decorating of grave sites. Still, Waterloo's affair took place two years later than Emily and Elizabeth's first meeting and one full year after their first planned gathering to honor the dead. Furthermore, the original Boalsburg event honored all the deceased, which is what Memorial Day has come to represent today.

So with respect to Waterloo and all twenty-two of the other claimants, it seems clear that Boalsburg, Pennsylvania, should be celebrated as having the very first Memorial Day. Today, one can participate in the annual fete there and watch the reenactment of the meeting of Emily Hunter, Sophie Keller, and Elizabeth Meyer as they strewed their flowers and mapped the future of a holiday celebrated and adored by all Americans.

The Handprint on the Wall

· 1877 ·

On June 21, 1877, Alexander Campbell is said to have rubbed his hand onto the dirty floor of the Carbon County Prison and placed his hand on the wall of cell block 17, leaving his print on the wall. He proclaimed that this handprint would be a perpetual symbol of his innocence and unwarranted death sentence. More than 120 years have passed and the handprint is still there to view. It has been washed over, painted over, plastered over, and dug out. Still, it remains there for all to see.

A former warden to the prison, Charles Neast, has been quoted as saying, "You don't believe it. I don't believe it. But there it is!"

Mr. Campbell claimed as he walked to the gallows that he was innocent of the crimes of which he was accused, and he had faith that God would preserve his handprint as a sign that he was indeed righteous. Campbell was accused of murder and of being part of the infamous group of Irish coal miners known as the Molly Maguires. The reputation of the Mollies was that they were all dangerous criminals. The Mollies were a clandestine group, so it is not known if they were all criminals. Campbell and three other men, all reputed to belong to the Mollies, were hanged that day in 1877. Joining Campbell on the gallows were Edward Kelly, Michael "Mickey" Doyle, and John "Yellow

Jack" Donohue. Campbell, Kelly, and Doyle had been convicted of the 1875 murder of mine boss John P. Jones of Lansford, Pennsylvania. Donohue was convicted of the murder of Morgan Powell, a Summit Hill mine boss in 1871.

In the 1860s there was big trouble in the coal fields of northeastern Pennsylvania. Working in the coal mines was an abysmal job with low pay and very dangerous working conditions. On top of that, the coal miners, most of whom were poor Irish immigrants, were being taken advantage of by the wealthy mine owners. The miners lived in company-owned houses and had to use their meager pay to purchase their mining supplies from the company store, the cost of which was deducted from their pay. The prices charged were not usually fair, but the miner who bought elsewhere soon found himself out of work. The result was that the miners were constantly in debt to the coal companies and therefore trapped in their jobs.

One more point of interest is that the real bosses were the railroad companies, since most of the mines were owned by the railroads through holding companies. This powerful group of men included Franklin B. Gowen of the Philadelphia & Reading Railroad Company, as well as Asa Packer of the Lehigh Valley Railroad, Sam Sloan of the Lackawanna Central of New Jersey, George Hayt of the Pennsylvania Coal Company, and Thomas Dickerson of the Delaware & Hudson Railroad. These men met in 1873 and "fixed" the price of coal at $5.00/ton. This was the very first case of price-fixing ever noted in the history of the United States.

As is the case in most disputes, bad deeds were committed by both sides. Once the miners were pushed hard enough, they fought back. Any resistance by the miners was considered an automatic association to the Mollies. Minor acts of rebellion such as work slowdowns were enough to get a miner lumped into the company of more dangerous individuals. It is difficult not to side with the miners, primarily because they were the underdogs. Additionally, everything they did to improve their condition was rapidly dealt a crippling blow. If a miner complained, he could get fired and then have his family put out on the street.

One big advantage that the mine owners had at that time was the use of James McParlan, a Pinkerton agent. Working in the mines under the name James McKenna, McParlan spent more than two years side by side with the miners, gaining their trust. However, he was no friend to the miners; unbeknownst to them, he reported to Franklin Gowen on the activities of the Mollies and directly caused the arrest and executions of many key people in that organization. The mine owners needed and wanted a slam dunk on these "ungrateful" mine workers in the courts. They felt that a speedy, successful trial would put all the other workers back in line. Their subsequent manipulation of the trial and punishment of the Mollies stands to this day as one of the greatest frauds ever perpetuated on the United States criminal system of justice.

Using information gathered by, and in some cases, manufactured by James McParlan and others planted inside the Molly Maguire organization, a private police force (also in the employ of the coal and railroad bosses) made their arrests. The prosecution team for the Commonwealth of Pennsylvania was led by General Charles Albright, a close personal friend of Asa Packer. Additionally, Frank W. Hughes became a member of the team. Mr. Hughes was the chief council for the Reading Railroad. Finally Franklin Gowen appointed himself to this prestigious group to round out the prosecutors. The only contributions from the state of Pennsylvania seem to be the courtroom and the gallows.

If the deck appeared to be stacked already, these powerful men were not yet finished. The last tool in their arsenal was the media. In essence, they owned it and were able to push their propaganda through it. Newspaper coverage went so far as to call for a conviction months before the trials even started. The newspaper coverage was not only biased, it was also plentiful.

Newspapers from all over the country sent reporters to the area. Seventy-nine percent of the 211 potential jurors claimed to have read all about the trials before they began. Seventy-two jurors were eventually seated for the trials. Of them, the only ones who hadn't heard of the trials were either illiterate or did not speak or understand English.

The convictions rolled in like clockwork. As men were charged with various crimes (mostly murder in the first degree) they were moved to the very modern state-of-the-art Carbon County Prison in Mauch Chunk.

On June 21, 1877, a special gallows was constructed in the main cell block to simultaneously hang the first four Mollies. Hundreds of spectators tried to fight their way inside. The cramped interior of the jail was full, and the streets outside were mobbed with spectators wanting to witness the hanging deaths of John Donohue, Michael Doyle, Alexander Campbell, and Edward Kelly. A few months later, on March 28, 1878, Thomas Fisher met the same fate, and on January 14, 1879, Charles Sharp and James McDonnell closed this chapter of history with their own deaths.

Historians agree that some of these men were in fact criminals. They may have been forced into their actions by the circumstances, but they were guilty nonetheless. Historians also agree that some of these men were probably innocent. They were likely caught in the net of the mine owners who were trying to bully the workers into submission. We will never know all the facts. Our only sign is a mysterious handprint and the accompanying legend that claims the mark was created by Campbell.

In 1975 the *National Inquirer* hired a geologist from Wilkes College in Wilkes-Barre, Pennsylvania, named Dr. Jeffrey T. Kline to conduct a scientific investigation into the mystery surrounding the handprint. Dr. Kline took samples of the handprint and the wall and analyzed them with a gas chromatograph, which is used to determine the chemical composition of organic materials. The findings showed no grease at all, only the chemical makeup of the paint. The doctor's conclusion was "If the print is not a grease mark, then there is no logical explanation for its persistence on the wall." Of course if the handprint were mere grease, a case could be made that someone was replenishing the handprint. So what is it? There is a handprint on the wall of cell block 17. In the words of the former warden, you don't believe it, I don't believe it, but there it is!

A Million-Dollar Baby Is Born

·1879·

Twenty-seven-year-old Frank Winfield Woolworth arrived in Lancaster, Pennsylvania, in 1879 with $30 and a dream. He arrived at dusk on May 30, tired and somewhat downtrodden from his recently failed business venture in Utica, New York. But the moment he stepped onto the streets of Lancaster, he felt the energy: "There was an amazing air of business and prosperity. Right away I felt that Lancaster was the place for me." That night he checked into an "old vile hotel" and the next morning began his search for a location to build his dream.

He found the perfect place, a 14-foot storefront on 170 North Queen Street. Putting his faith in his dream, he made arrangements to rent it for $30 a month.

With his lease in hand, he quickly returned home to Watertown, New York, and gathered up his pregnant wife, Jennie, and his four-year-old daughter, Helena, to embark on this adventure.

He had also gotten both the blessing of and a $300 loan from his previous boss, William Moore. With that money he paid the rent on his new building, had the excess merchandise from his failed store in Utica shipped over to Lancaster, and bought more supplies.

For the next several days he worked nonstop, as did the seven clerks he had hired. He prominently displayed a card in the window of his Utica shop, which read NOTHING OVER 5 CENTS. Interest was aroused, and the local Amish farmers and other town residents eagerly awaited the opening.

This was Woolworth's only advertising, for Frank did not have the money for nor the faith in paid advertising. He believed in word of mouth and the occasional flyer, a practice that his company continued for decades to come.

The night before the grand opening, Frank and Jennie couldn't sleep. It hadn't been an easy road that led to this day in 1879.

Born on a farm in Rodman, New York, in 1851, Frank started doing farm chores at the age of four. Seven years later, when his family moved to a 108-acre farm in Champion, New York, Frank and his younger brother Charles were actively working the farm side by side with their dad, John, a potato farmer. The family was dirt poor.

The only thing Frank looked forward to was his school lessons, which were about to end; farm boys were only schooled until age sixteen. He loved history and was obsessed with Napoleon Bonaparte. It was from reading about Bonaparte's life he learned the secret to success: You have to have a dream, a plan, and the determination to never quit. Frank remembered the shabby treatment he and his father got from store owners on trips into town to buy farm supplies. He vowed he would one day have a store that would sell quality goods at a price that all people could afford and that all customers would be treated with respect.

As Frank grew up, he told his mom about his dream. She gave him her life savings of twelve dollars, which was just enough for him to take a two-month course at a business school. Frank earned a diploma, but he was laughed at by the wealthy merchants when he applied for a job dressed in farm rags, holding a diploma. For several years he went back to working the plow and getting up at four in the morning to shovel manure. He was discouraged, but he never gave up asking store merchants any chance he could for a job.

Finally one man, William Moore, saw the determination in Frank and decided to give him a job. Moore's offer included a six-month trial period without pay. Frank negotiated the trial down to three months and a deal was set. He was hired by Augsbury & Moore's Corner Store in Watertown, New York, in 1873. It was a favor that Frank never forgot and paid back many times over, making Moore a millionaire later in life.

Frank tried his hand at selling but was dubbed the worst salesman the store ever had; however, his charm and determination won Moore over once again, and he decided to keep Frank in the store.

Then one fine day in September of 1878, a salesman came into Moore's store and told him about a store in Michigan that put together a table of hard-to-sell items, all priced at 5 cents, and sold them. Intrigued, Moore told Frank to put together a 5-cent display table, and by morning a beautiful table with bright red ribbons was on hand. The table was a success and sold out in a matter of hours. At that moment Frank's idea crystallized: He would open not just any store, but a 5-cent store, and a whole chain of them at that.

In February of 1879, Frank opened his first store in Utica, but it failed three months later because he had chosen a poor location. But Frank followed the tip of another salesman and tried his second store in Lancaster, which opened on June 21, 1879. If he had a crystal ball, he would have known he was about to give birth to a million-dollar baby.

But for now he was just having intense labor pains as Saturday morning arrived. There was a huge crowd already peering in the front window. Excited, Frank headed for the door, but his fifteen-year-old clerk Charles Hoffmeier beat him to it and thus went down in history as letting the first patron into the store. Hundreds followed behind him, pushing their way to the display tables.

Frank had carefully picked a variety of items that fit in with the simple lifestyles of the Amish and Mennonites who would make up the bulk of his patrons. Customers surrounded the tables overflowing with toy dustpans, tin pepper boxes, purses, biscuit cutters, candlesticks, flea soap, flour dredges, school straps, skimmers, apple covers, sadiron stands, fire shovels, stamped-in cups, ABC plates, lather brushes, pencil charms, police whistles, red jewelry, and turkey red napkins. And everything cost only 5 cents!

People were in awe that they didn't have to ask or haggle for the price, a practice that was common in those days, as all items in stores back then were unmarked. They also liked that they could look at the merchandise themselves and weren't followed around by a clerk, another first for their time. And Frank kept his promise; all the customers were treated very kindly, a thing that some of them had never experienced while shopping.

Yes, Frank Woolworth not only created a new kind of store, he revolutionized the way that people shopped. Frank had the business sense to know you have to make items visually appealing. So he had put bright red fabric around the items. He instinctively knew what the big merchandising giants of today know—the color red psychologically entices people to buy.

Although he was very excited, Frank was not naive. He was only making a penny or two on each item, so every penny counted. After each sale was made, the clerks had to walk to the back of the store to Mr. Woolworth himself to get change. Every amount was recorded on a tablet. To make his money stretch, Frank had his clerks wrap the customers' items in used local newspapers, because the regular brown wrapping paper cost a whopping 8 cents a pound, which was out of his league for now.

That first night the store closed at 11:00 P.M. when the last customer left. Frank tallied up his totals. Jennie held her breath waiting for the final results, and finally Frank turned to her with a big smile. He had sold 30 percent of his stock at $127.65. He knew he had a winner on his hands.

As the weeks passed, word spread throughout the countryside, and Frank's business was booming. But he had run into a problem. It was time to restock, and he was out of cash since he had promptly paid Mr. Moore back with every nickel that came in. This time it was his landlady, Mrs. Kendig, who loaned him $200 to buy more merchandise. With that loan Frank was able to get the store running on its own. Frank never forgot his landlady. He not only paid her back; for every month till the day she died, he gave her $200. Frank never forgot anyone who believed in him from the start, and anyone who partnered with him later became a millionaire.

With the success of his Lancaster store, Frank Woolworth opened twelve more. He expanded the concept to include items costing 10 cents, and thus was born the "five and ten" store, later coined the "five and dime." Some stores failed and other succeeded. When something failed, Frank merely said he was "regrouping."

The "King of Five and Dimes" worked night and day, and the Woolworth empire grew. There were Woolworth's in Cuba, Germany, Hawaii, Mexico, Puerto Rico, Spain, the Virgin Islands, France, Great Britain, and Canada. The "red fronts" as they were called, due to their big, bold, red storefront letters, were the first, the largest, and the most famous five-and-dime stores in history.

People around the world have fond memories of either having a grilled cheese sandwich, an egg cream, or hot turkey dinner at the counter with the swivel red leather seats, all for 10 cents. Others remember buying their first turtle, goldfish, or parakeet in Woolworth's. Still others remember the perfumes or jewelry they could buy on the first-ever layaway plan.

Frank never forgot the birthplace of his business. He went back to Lancaster years later and built a new five-story Woolworth skyscraper on the corner of North Queen and Grant. This magnificent Woolworth's had an exotic roof-garden "refreshment room," complete with a vaudeville house where customers could watch singers, comedians, and acrobats.

Woolworth's became an icon and worked its way into the American culture. It was written about in poems and songs, was mentioned in Broadway shows, and even made it onto the silver screen. Frank also went on to construct the Woolworth Building in New York City, which was the world's tallest edifice from 1913 to 1930. He paid for the construction of this sixty-story "Cathedral of Commerce" with $13.2 million in cash, making it the only skyscraper in the world, past or present, completely unencumbered by debt or mortgage. Woolworth's was also the scene of a truly historic moment in American history: The lunch counter at the Woolworth's in Greensboro, North Carolina, was the first desegregated restaurant in the country. On February 1, 1960, at 4:30 P.M. four African American college students, later dubbed the "Four Freshmen" walked into the Woolworth store and asked for a cup of coffee. At first they weren't served, but after several "sit-ins" the story made national headlines. Against neighborhood wishes, Woolworth's decided to serve them and established its new slogan, "Everybody's Stores." It changed America. The original lunch counter is on display at the Smithsonian Institute in Washington, D.C., as a reminder of the end of segregation.

The Woolworth's stores survived for 118 years. On July 17, 1997, the corporation announced that they would be changing their name and closing all Woolworth's in the United States forever—all 7,000 of them, employing well over a million people.

Frank Woolworth proved the American dream—that millions can be made from nickels and dimes if you never give up.

Punxsutawney Phil: The Whole Truth about the Groundhog

· 1887 ·

Bright and early on the morning of February 2, 1887, the official gathering of the Punxsutawney Groundhog Club made its first historic journey up to Gobbler's Knob. The club was comprised of local businessmen, groundhog hunters, and town folk. Their fearless leader and founder was Clymer Freas, editor of the local newspaper, *The Punxsutawney Spirit.*

The purpose of the trek was to determine if "Punxsutawney Phil," the now-famous weather-forecasting groundhog, would see his shadow. Legend has it that if the groundhog should emerge from his hole on February 2 and see his shadow, winter will last another cold and snowy six weeks, at least. If, on the other hand, the day is bleak and cloudy so that no shadow appears, the frosty season should be near its end.

This February day in 1887 had few clouds and abundant sunshine, and so it was duly recorded in *The Punxsutawney Spirit* that Phil did indeed see his shadow and everyone should prepare for a long chilly spell.

The question that comes immediately to mind is why did Clymer Freas decide to use this rodent and this day to predict his local weather in this particular manner? Believe it or not, the answer comes from a combination of diverse European customs and early American Indian traditions.

The town of Punxsutawney lies about 80 miles northeast of Pittsburgh in the Allegheny Mountains. The early settlers to the area were from numerous European countries including Germany, England, France, and parts of Scandinavia. The English had an old song attached to a minor holiday called Candlemas Day, which was celebrated by having leaders from various churches bless candles and pass them out to their congregations. The song loosely ties the Candlemas holiday to the weather.

> If Candlemas be fair and bright,
> Come, winter, have another flight.
> If Candlemas brings cold and rain,
> Go, winter, and come not again.

There lies the heart of Groundhog Day: an ancient ritualistic holiday that is tied to weather predictions. Candlemas is the root, but how did it evolve, and why the groundhog? Who brought that to the mix? Long, long ago the Germans picked up pieces of the Candlemas holiday, and for some reason, the Germans added the use of a hedgehog as a symbolic shadow caster. Perhaps it was believed that hedgehogs were among the first of the hibernating animals to appear each year. Whatever the reason, this was the animal that Germans associated with hopes for an early spring.

When the German settlers came to northwestern Pennsylvania, they had immediate interaction with the native Lenni-Lenape Indians. While there were no hedgehogs to be found anywhere in North America, groundhogs, also called woodchucks, were plentiful. In fact local Indians revered the animal. Much like the Germans with their hedgehog, Indians believed the woodchuck had special powers and abilities. They even gave us the name woodchuck. The Indian word for the animal was *oijik*, pronounced variously as *wejak* or *wojak,* which became Americanized as woodchuck. The Germans deemed this a good replacement for their own beloved hedgehog.

This comprises most of the ingredients for our little "groundhog stew." Now it is time to add Chinese astronomy and the Babylonian Calendar. Both Chinese astronomy and the Babylonian Calendar point to approximately February 2 as the midwinter point. Midwinter is precisely when most farmers started dreaming of a possible early spring. Of course in Pennsylvania and other northern climates, farmers are a bit more realistic than to expect an early end to winter. In farming circles it isn't unusual to hear the famous saying, "Groundhog Day— Half your hay." This was to imply that a reasonable farmer would still have half his resources left to be able to provide for his animals during the long winter months yet to come.

All of these factors, from Candlemas to hedgehogs to Chinese astronomy, came together to form our present-day version of Groundhog Day. The next question is why in the world did Clymer Freas make such a big deal about it? Perhaps it was partly for fun, gathering the boys for an early morning hike to play with a groundhog. We do know that Clymer was also interested in promoting the sleepy little town of Punxsutawney. Perhaps he figured that if more and more people talked about Groundhog Day, and specifically Punxsutawney Phil, that he might be able to attract new interest in the area.

His plan was a success almost from the beginning. Each year the fame of Punxsutawney Phil grew. Once the Pittsburgh press got hold of the story, it blossomed farther and faster. Little by little, more tradition and fun were added to the event. Phil even got outfitted with a wordy nickname, "The Seer of Seers, Sage of Sages, Prognosticator of Prognosticators, and Weather Prophet Extraordinary." Punxsutawney is sometimes referred to as the "The Weather Capital of the World." Throughout the past century, the crowds on Gobbler's Knob got bigger and bigger. When television got involved, Punxsutawney really got on the map. The event was first broadcast coast-to-coast on NBC's morning television show with Dave Garroway. Soon all media covered the event. Newspapers, TV, and radio sent reporters to Punxsutawney, helping to create the carnival atmosphere that surrounds the all-important moment when Phil is brought out of his burrow to make his forecast.

In the 1980s Punxsutawney Phil took a road trip and met with President Ronald Reagan. In addition, a couple of governors of Pennsylvania have joined the Groundhog Club for the festivities over the years.

Hollywood added much of the pizzazz when it released the movie *Groundhog Day,* starring Bill Murray and costarring the one-and-only Phil. The film was such a success that now thousands upon thousands of people descend on this little community every year to celebrate and rejoice with the groundhog. Fireworks, formal balls, ice sculptures, and games are all part of the merriment. The Punxsutawney Groundhog Club actually dresses up in formal wear for the early morning event.

Is the groundhog an accurate predictor of the weather? Well, no, not really. He has been correct about 35 percent of the time. Of course no one in Punxsutawney likes to dwell on this point, nor do they like to acknowledge that the life expectancy for the average groundhog is unlikely to exceed the one-hundred-plus years of Phil's existence, claiming instead that the current Phil is the original groundhog. Perhaps the answer to the question of Phil's longevity lies in his plush digs: He resides in a dandy climate-controlled burrow right in the library in downtown Punxsutawney. Visitors are welcome any time of the year.

If his long life is not due to these sumptuous surroundings, then maybe he is a magical reincarnated Lenni-Lanape Indian. After all, how many groundhogs do you know that have visited with presidents, governors, and movie stars? For that matter, how many groundhogs could start out with a bunch of groundhog hunters and avoid becoming a main dish?

The bottom line is that Groundhog Day is a unique and special day. There are other pretenders to the Groundhog Day throne, but none has the staying power or fame of "The Seer of Seers, Sage of Sages, Prognosticator of Prognosticators, and Weather Prophet Extraordinary"—the one, the only, Punxsutawney Phil—the same groundhog that Clymer Freas found and named in February 1887, in Punxsutawney, Pennsylvania.

Water, Water Everywhere and Way Too Much to Drink

·1889·

By May 31, 1889, it had been raining heavily for three consecutive days. The city of Johnstown, Pennsylvania, was already flooded, but that was nothing new. Johnstown was and still is prone to flooding. It is surrounded on three sides by mountains and has at its town center the junction of the Little Conemaugh River and Stony Creek, which meet to form the Conemaugh River. The configuration of the mountains and the rivers makes Johnstown a natural disaster waiting to happen.

On this May day, the minor flooding, which the residents feared but controlled throughout the years, was not the real problem. However, 14 miles north of Johnstown atop a mountain, a monster lay in wait. On top of this mountain was the wide expanse of a man-made lake known as Lake Conemaugh, the main attraction of the beautiful South Fork Fishing and Hunting Club, a tony resort for the rich and famous. One of the most prominent owners was the steel tycoon Andrew Carnegie of Pittsburgh. The peaceful lake did not give a hint of its monstrous power.

Early on the morning of May 31, Colonel Elias J. Unger, the property manager of the South Fork Fishing and Hunting Club, realized the lake's water level was rising at an alarming rate. He estimated the increase at 4 to 6 inches per hour. At that rate the water would crest the breast of the dam in a few short hours. Unger knew what would happen when the water started to pass over the top of an earthen dam. The erosion would be very quick. He immediately enlisted the help of a few employees, including the club's resident engineer, John Parke. Together they attempted to raise the wall of the dam with little effect. Unger then sent for a group of Italian workers who were in the area building new sewers. These men were employed to dig a new spillway.

By 11:00 A.M. it became apparent that their work was in vain. The colonel dispatched young Mr. Parke down to the village of South Fork to send a warning. Mr. Parke rode his horse 2 miles and spread a frantic message to clear the village and pass the word. A telegraph message was sent and the warning went out. "Run for your lives. The dam is breaking!"

To the detriment of thousands, most took this warning very lightly. For years the caveat had been a running joke, with locals slipping off a lighthearted remark just like the one John Parke yelled. Years of living under this threat had made the warning impotent.

John Parke made the trek back to the dam site to continue the futile efforts of holding back the beastly waters. Lake Conemaugh was approximately 2 miles long and as much as a mile wide in some places. The dam itself was over 900 feet wide and 72 feet high. It was estimated to contain 20 million tons of water.

At 3:00 P.M. the water started spilling over the top of the dam. Immediately the breastworks started to give way. The old earthen dam was no match for that amount of contained fury. In less than one hour the hundreds of spectators who had gathered witnessed the complete draining of what was at the time one of the largest man-made lakes in the world.

Eyewitness accounts describe the event as a 30-foot wall of water and debris. This giant, forceful wave simply crushed everything in its unswerving path. The houses and villages

were completely uprooted and destroyed. Anything and everything in the path actually became part of its destructive force.
Timber and stone became solid projectiles battering all that lay
before the maelstrom.

As the beast approached the city, it carried houses, barns,
and animals, dead and alive. It contained portions of the small
towns it destroyed along the way. The communities of South
Fork, Mineral Point, Woodvale, and East Conemaugh were
heavily represented in the carnage. One last obstacle attempted
to quell its fury: an old stone railroad bridge. This massive
structure was built to allow trains to cross from one end of the
valley to the other. Amazingly, the bridge did not fall, and it
also stopped much of the debris being carried by the on-
slaught. Despite the temporary relief, in the long run this would
prove to be even more frightening and devastating than imagination can bear.

While the bridge did not collapse, neither did it stop the
assault of the water. The wall of water continued on to destroy
the entire city of Johnstown. Then, as it plowed into the far
mountain, it simply folded back on itself and made a new pass
at the dismantled city. All the debris now was pushed back
against the old stone bridge. The few survivors that floundered
in the water or clung to some self-made life raft were about to
face the unthinkable.

Johnstown was a modern city of the time, built with gas
pipes to light the streets and many of the homes. This system
of pipes was now mangled beyond recognition. It only took
one stray spark to ignite the area around the stone bridge.
Within seconds what was once a disaster became a calamity. A
raging inferno erupted and most efforts to save survivors were
stopped dead in their tracks. Many people stood on the hills
and watched in horror.

Stories of heroes and heroic deeds abound. Perhaps one
of the most touching is the story of six-year-old Gertrude Quinn
Slattery. Caught out in the waters clinging to a mud-soaked

mattress, she screamed and pleaded for help. A group of people floating on a nearby portion of a rooftop heard the agonizing pleas for help. Despite attempts to restrain him, Maxwell McAchren plunged into the raging waters and swam to her rescue. After gaining a perch on the limp bedding, Mr. McAchren picked up Gertrude and threw the child to those he had left on the floating rooftop and to safety. Most others caught in the melee were not so fortunate.

In just a few short hours, 2,209 lives were lost. Remnants of the wreckage were found as far away as Steubenville, Ohio, a distance of 120 miles! The devastation was complete. The city of Johnstown had few buildings left standing. More than 1,600 homes were lost.

In all, 777 bodies were recovered with no identification. These poor souls were laid to rest in a special section of Grandview Cemetery. Located high on the mountain in the borough of Westmont is a beautifully designed plot with 777 individual headstones and a large monument at the front. The inscription reads, IN MEMORY OF THE UNIDENTIFIED DEAD FROM THE FLOOD MAY 31ST, 1889.

The monument featuring an angel pointing to the heavens was dedicated on May 31, 1892. More than 10,000 members of the community gathered with the governor of Pennsylvania, Robert Emory Pattison, for the unveiling. Speeches were given and prayers were offered. When the moment arrived, the tarp covering the monument was pulled aside, and just as it slid away, a bird fluttered to the up-stretched finger of the angelic monument. The bird perched directly on the finger as a collective gasp escaped the throats of the onlookers. Perhaps this small event helped to give the people of Johnstown the hope to go on with their lives.

The South Fork Dam was never rebuilt. Johnstown still floods from time to time, with deadly floods in both 1936 and 1977. However, the people of Johnstown are of hardy stock. They rebuild and go on with their lives.

Tragedy at 700 Feet Below
·1911·

The early morning of April 7 started out like any other work-day as 350 men and boys trudged to the Price-Pancoast Mine in Throop to earn their meager living. The miners on contract were paid $2.50 a week, and day laborers were paid $2.00 a week. In small groups they were lowered by shafts into the mines and would work in the various tunnels according to their assignments for the day.

On this particular morning, more than seventy men walked the wooden gangways and made their way into the deep chambers of the China vein, 700 feet below the surface, to dig for coal. The China vein was a blind tunnel, meaning it was a tunnel with only one exit that wasn't visible from where the men were working.

On duty that day was James Moore, a slope engineer, whose job was to attend to both the west slope engine house and the north slope engine house. He would alternate between the two to make sure they were running smoothly.

Around 9:00 A.M., while Moore was inspecting the west side, a small fire started on the north side, which was the con-verging point between the Dunmore vein and the China vein. Moore saw the smoke, grabbed a group of men, and ran to douse the flames.

An inside foreman by the name of Walter Knight saw what was happening. He and the fire boss Isaac Dawe grabbed some "pipemen" and tried to put the fire out as well.

The engine house wasn't exactly a house but rather a wooden platform with a wooden windshield and roof. Because it was made of wood, the flames were spreading along the wooden props and down the 300-foot-long double timbers that served as the gangway straight toward the China vein.

The ventilation fans, which were constantly circulating in the mines, were feeding the flames and pushing them down the tunnel. The seventy men inside the blind China tunnel were unaware of the fire looming just 2,000 feet from them. However, Knight and Dawe saw the danger and ran towards the China tunnel to warn the men. On the way they met one of their bosses, John R. Perry, who was with a laborer. Knight told Perry about the fire. Perry told his laborer to get out at once and then he joined Knight and Dawe as they raced to warn the men.

Once outside, the laborer told the colliery officials what was happening. However, the aboveground officials underestimated the fire and figured the men below could handle it; they did not call a halt to operations. Down below, the smoke was building.

Meanwhile in the mine, Knight, Dawe, and Perry had reached the men in the China vein, but as they all began to run out of the mine, they were stopped by the intense heat and smoke at the only exit, which was now blocked by the fire.

They were now trapped in the tunnel. Men wrapped their shirts around their heads, hoping to breathe. With the smoke getting worse, those on the surface realized the fire was out of hand and sent out a fire call, which brought the Dickson City Hose Company, located a mile from the mine, to the scene. They lowered a 500-foot hose line into the shaft, but it burst from the pressure. They quickly called for more backup and tried to locate other hoses. Inside the men were now dropping from smoke inhalation. Those at the surface knew the situation was grim. It was impossible to keep the smoke away from the trapped men. The only way to stop it was to turn off the ventilation fans, but then the trapped men would be at the mercy of the gases, which would build up and explode if the fans were turned off, leading to certain death. They reluctantly kept the fans on and hoped they could put the fire out in time so the men would have a chance to get out.

By noon, C. E. Tobey, an assistant general superintendent of the Delaware and Lackawanna Western Coal Department, arrived on the scene and was told that men were trapped on the other side of the fire. By now the fire had spread along the gangway, over twenty empty mine cars. The smoke was brutal. The support beam timbers were on fire now and the water hoses that had entered the mines were rubbing against the cave roof and cracking the heated rocks, which caused them to chip and fall in layers.

Tobey took it upon himself to call in other rescue crews from surrounding areas. Other hoses were obtained and two streams of water were pumped in. Finally they got the fire under control. But it still wasn't enough to get to the men yet.

While Tobey and others were orchestrating the relief efforts, the men not caught in the China vein were still being hoisted out of the mines in groups of ten. They estimated that about seventy-five people were trapped, sixty-five men and ten boys.

Word was spreading around town. By 2:30 P.M. hundreds of the wives and children of the miners had arrived and were standing by the shaft. A makeshift rope was stretched around the shaft to keep the crowd in control. Shortly after 3:00 P.M. a rescue crew of twelve men arrived. The rescue team only got as far as the burned engine house when they found the first three victims. Their bodies were face down and they were covering their faces. Sadly, they took the bodies to the foot of the shaft one by one.

The rescue team went back to look for more survivors and instead found more dead bodies. By this point they figured that everyone in the China vein section was dead, but they were determined to keep on trying. However, the smoke and heat was so intense even with the fire out that they reeled back and fell and needed stimulants just to keep conscious. As one surviving miner, from the upper portion of the mine, put it as he came out of the mineshaft, "What shot have these men got? What chance have they got when the rescuers themselves are falling over? They're all dead. No man can live down there."

By 4:15 the fire was completely out. It had burned for approximately seven hours.

At 4:40 a doctor by the name of Jacobs entered the mine. Twenty minutes later he was hoisted up, calling for blankets and whiskey, and a volunteer promptly ran 2 blocks to get the supplies. The blankets were to cover the dead, and the whiskey was to revive the living.

By now a crowd of 5,000 people had gathered. The local coroners were waiting around like jackals, all fighting to get the best position for the huge task that was ahead of them. At a time like this, they saw dollar bills instead of humans in their eyes. The undertakers were later condemned by officials for their "ghoulish tactics," which included paying friends to accompany them to the morgue and claim the body was that of a relative, just so the undertaker could get the body and collect the fee.

A decision was made not to take any bodies out of the mine in daylight in front of the crowd. Instead they were laid in blankets by the foot of the shaft. The rescuers found twenty-one bodies by midnight. The bodies farthest in were those of the foreman, Walter Knight, and the fire boss, Isaac Dawe, who ran into the tunnel and attempted to get the men out ahead of themselves. The victims that were found were in groups of three and five, all lying face down in the ditches, with handkerchiefs pressed against their faces indicating that they fought hard to fight off suffocation.

After dark, the bodies were brought to the surface one or two at a time in the mine carriage. A bell would tinkle four times to signal that the carriage needed to be lifted. The engine would start up, clang and roar, and bring the corpses to the surface. After the body was identified, it was marked with an identification slip, then the name of the victim was whispered from person to person (as in a game of telephone) as the coroner took them away, so as not to upset the family members by just calling it out.

By 3:00 A.M. thirty-five bodies had been hoisted up, and they were still coming. In the end, seventy-two miners and one rescue worker died, ranging in age from sixteen to seventy. The disaster left fifty-six women widows and 123 children fatherless. It was the worst mining tragedy in the history of northern Pennsylvania.

Naturally no one wanted to take the blame. Company officials were accused of violating safety laws, which they denied, and said they would allow an investigation. Some officials laid blame on the men, saying they panicked in the mine and could have gotten out. Regardless of what caused the tragedy, the result was the same: Within six days after the disaster, the China vein was cleared and back in business. Once again those needing to make a living went back into the maze of tunnels and began digging.

There was no such thing as compensation for widows or orphans, so people went door-to-door to collect for the families, and a large public fund-raiser called the "keg fund" was held throughout the country for the survivors. Individuals, churches, and businesses raised $70,000 in the relief effort, and the funds were distributed by the Anthracite Trust company.

The tremendous impact of the disaster brought about new legislation. An act was passed that mandated that to save the lives of future miners and to protect and preserve property, all inside buildings (engine houses, pump houses, and stables, etc.) must be constructed of incombustible material. Failure to comply would result in heavy fines. It was also strongly suggested that two escape paths must be provided. All mines had six months after the approval of the act to comply. Today seventeen historical markers stand throughout Lackawanna County, marking where miners died. A permanent marker is to be placed in Throop as a reminder of the significance of the disaster that claimed those lives and the subsequent passage of the legislation that makes mining safer for those underground.

Fill 'er Up:
Convenience on
the Road

· 1913 ·

In every city in this country, in every country in the civilized world, there are drive-in gas stations. But it wasn't always like that. Picture this. A century ago, you might have been driving your car and noticed it was running low on gas. In order to fill up, you would have had to look around for a hardware store or some kind of general store that dispensed petroleum products. Once you found a store, you then would have had to go around to the back and find someone who was available to help you pump the gasoline. Finally you could drive away. This was great if you had all the time in the world, but not so good if you were in a rush, or your car needed a quick lube job or a flat tire fixed.

But that all changed on December 1, 1913, when the Gulf Refining Company opened the world's first *drive-in* service station, located on the corner of Baum Boulevard and St. Clair Street in Pittsburgh, about 1 mile from the University of Pittsburgh campus. This wasn't the first gas station, but the first drive-in service station constructed specifically for convenience.

Now that drive-in gas stations are commonplace, it doesn't seem like it should have been such a hard idea to come up with.

But until then, people just didn't think cars were important or common enough to warrant their own gas facility. It seemed as silly to them as the idea of bottled water was to us when it first came out. (What? Pay for water? There's no need for it. I can just go home and drink it from my tap.)

At the time, cars were just a newfangled machine, a fancy toy owned by only the very wealthy. But once Gulf realized that people were using their cars more and becoming more dependent on them, they wanted to make it as easy as possible for people to purchase the very thing that made their cars go: gas.

So the Gulf Company leased a property from James R. Mellon and family. They paid a mere $16 a month for the first year, with the understanding that they were going to build a service station. Next Gulf hired J. H. Giesey, an architect already employed by the wealthy Mellon family. Together Giesey and the Gulf Refining Company agreed on a design for the building. Since no building had ever been built for this purpose, they worked hard at looking ahead to the needs of the employees and the motorists. The small building they designed would offer shelter for the employees, a storage room for sales records, and a space to store lube oil. It also had a single restroom for employee use. Once the blueprints were finalized, Gulf brought in H. S. Moorhead & Company to do the construction. The project was started in the summer. Even though it was a small building, it took a few months to complete because they had difficulty setting the pilings of the building in the sandy soil in a way that could support the wide canopy of the building. When the stabilization problem was finally solved, they were ready for a grand opening in December. As Bob Beck, co-founder of the Gulf Historical Society, said recently, "With today's technology the *Monster Garage* guys could have built it in a day, but back then it was a major project."

As completion day drew near, Gulf sent out invitations to all of the automobile owners in the neighborhood, announcing the opening of the first-of-its-kind service station and encouraging them to be a part of history.

At exactly 7:00 A.M. on that December day, the world's first service station opened. The manager, Frank McLaughlin, flicked a switch, and a big sign on the front of the building lit up with GOOD GULF GASOLINE and SUPREME AUTO OIL. The letters were formed with the most modern lightbulbs of the day so the sign could be illuminated at night and seen from great distances.

The newly built pagoda-style building stood waiting majestically for the stream of customers. It was a two-tone building with handsome dark red brick walls on the lower half of the building. The top half had several windows, and on one of the windows there was a wooden sign that read, GOOD GULF GASOLINE 27 CENTS PER GALLON. A canopy overhang with lighting extended out 42 feet wide so that the attendants and patrons could be protected from rain or snow while filling up their cars. On hand to attend the patrons that day were the manager and four uniformed, eager attendants. The first car to arrive was a Model T Ford, which probably cost about $400 brand new. The driver was the first to receive service and experience the most modern and accurate gasoline delivery system of the time, the Bowser Delivery System, which had the state-of-the-art red, sentry-type (meaning it stood straight up like a sentry soldier) hand-crank pumps. This was indeed spiffy, especially compared to the dispensers from local stores at the time, which offered wooden drums with wooden spigots hammered into the side. The first service station patron drove off both happy and impressed.

Others pulled up in their Model Ts (there was not a large variety of cars in those days) and were offered full service, which included free crankcase service, air, water, and installation of tires and tubes if needed. Most, however, just bought gas. A slow stream of customers came in that day, but Gulf knew Rome wasn't built in a day. Besides, all those who did come in felt that the station was truly a driver's paradise.

At the end of the first day, 30 gallons of gas had been sold. Word quickly spread. The next day 32 gallons were sold, and by the end of the week, on that first Saturday, they sold 350 gallons. The Gulf Company knew they had a winner. This small gas station in Pennsylvania quickly served as the model for service stations around the nation and the world.

Gas companies began competing to build flashier and bigger stations. Everyone wanted to get on the bandwagon, but Gulf was clearly in the lead. It was the beginning of a never-ending project to develop bigger and better stations to attract and serve the customers.

The Gulf Oil Company went on to pioneer many other firsts with this service station. They were the first to come up with the idea of free restrooms, which were available to patrons at these stations, and which so many of us use today during long road trips. They also came up with free road maps produced by the Gulf Company itself in 1914. The maps, as well as the offer of free air for tires, were used as marketing tools to entice patrons to come into the station.

In July of 2000 the Gulf Oil Historical Society, recognizing the invention of something that changed the way the nation operates, erected a yellow and blue marker on the site of the first station. The marker reads, "At this site in Dec. 1913, Gulf Refining Co. opened the first drive-in facility designed and built to provide gasoline, oils & lubricants to the motoring public. Its success led to construction of thousands of gas stations by different oil companies across the nation."

The original drive-in service station is now long gone, and its site is now a vacant lot that is used for parking. But if you look closely, you can see that the cracks in the asphalt of the parking lot match the concrete slabs that are shown in the historical photos on display of the original gas station, which can be viewed on the Gulf Oil Historical Society's Web site.

Now the next time you drive up to a service station on a cold day and have the attendant wash your windows and fill up your car, while you run in to use the restroom, you can smile knowing where it all started. And as you get back in your car, you can be thankful that you don't have to get your gas inside a Home Depot instead.

The First Armored Car Robbery in History

· 1927 ·

It seemed like a routine Friday. Two Brink's armored cars were doing the payroll rounds for Pittsburgh Terminal Coal Company in western Pennsylvania. Inside the truck was $103,834.38, the pay for the miners for the last two weeks of February. The money had been taken from the office of the Brink's Express company in the morning and was being dropped off at each mine so the workers could be paid. The front armored car carried the loot, while the rear car carried five armed guards. They had just dropped off $70,000 at the number two and number three mines and were heading with the remainder of the cash to three other mines. It was just about noon and they were right on schedule. Little did they know they were about to become part of history.

Paul Jawarski and eight other members of his notorious Flatheads gang were lying in wait up ahead of the trucks. The Flatheads, so named because of the shape of Jawarski's head, were crouching patiently out of sight behind a fallen tree 100 yards from Old Bethel Road near Coverdale, waiting for the armored cars to pass. Beside them was a battery with 100 yards of electric lines. Those electric lines were connected to two underground dynamite charges placed 60 feet apart. In just a few minutes, they would attempt the nation's first armored car robbery.

As the Brink's trucks turned onto Liberty Road and headed to the next coal mine, a subterranean blast ripped through the street, creating a 60-foot-wide mass of holes and mud. With precision timing, the blast exploded the moment the first car passed over it. It was a direct hit. It lifted the armored car into the air and threw it 75 feet away, flipping it on its roof and leaving the driver unconscious. Moments later a second explosion occurred. It missed the second armored car filled with guards but created another series of huge holes. The force of that explosion tossed the second car onto its side and into one of the craterlike holes. All five guards were knocked unconscious.

The Flatheads lost no time. They quickly scrambled out of hiding and ran over to the damaged vehicles. They trampled over the unconscious victims and frantically scooped up the 1,700 scattered payroll envelopes containing exactly $103,834.38 in loot. Just as they had discussed, some bandits stood watch over the unconscious men, while the others gathered the money.

William Tarr, the driver of the first car, was the first to regain consciousness, but a bandit ordered him to keep quiet. As some of the other payroll guards regained consciousness, the bandits pointed their guns at them and told them to "roll over and keep their faces down in the mud."

As the Flatheads finished scooping up the money and hopped into their getaway vehicle, Tarr bravely looked up. He got a clear look at one of the members and managed to get the make and license plate number of the getaway car as it sped away. It was a blue Stearns-Knight with Pennsylvania plate number 602-595.

As soon as the gang left the scene, the guards wrangled themselves from the wreckage and assisted the others who were injured. With no other way of calling for help, the guards staggered as a group to the nearest mine. Since the telephone lines were damaged during the blast, they weren't able to get to the police right away.

Thirty minutes later, when the police were finally alerted, they immediately leapt into action. The guards were all rushed to St. Joseph's Hospital. Two men had been critically injured, with severe lacerations to the head and body. Those not seriously injured gave their accounts to the police, and the police immediately put out an all points bulletin (APB).

Based on two tips from underworld sources, one squad of detectives scoured the hills near Coraopolis for an Italian gang leader who was said to have been seen making several trips to Pittsburgh a few weeks before and flashing money around, apparently trying to round up a gang for the robbery. Another squad searched Library Road armed with riot guns in response to information that the gang had a machine gun in the getaway vehicle. Unfortunately, the gang was nowhere to be found. Despite the tips, the gang managed to evade scores of police and detectives who tried to trail them through Washington and Allegheny Counties.

With the half-hour lead time, the robbers were laughing their way to freedom. The police had lost their trail for now. But at least they had the plate number, which they traced to J. A. Gilmore of Washington Heights. But Gilmore sent a telegram to the police stating that his car had not been stolen and was in fact in his garage at the present time.

Early the next morning, Saturday, March 12, a clue was picked up in Bentleyville, Washington County, when a woman called the police station to report seeing a car like the bandits' speed past her home. Using that information along with another tip from a secret source, Chief George Murren took the county detectives and police with him and went to Joe Weckoski's farm 3 miles from Bentleyville. They hit the jackpot. There in the midst of piled-up hay were three soundly sleeping suspects,

Stanley Stanko of Detroit, Stanley Melowski of Glassport, and the gang leader, Paul Jawarski.

The cops had been looking for Jawarski for a long time. The Flatheads gang had staged a series of violent holdups in Pennsylvania, Ohio, and Michigan throughout the 1920s that netted them about $200,000. The crimes had left several victims dead. Jawarski himself boasted of killing twenty-six men. He had been sentenced to die in the electric chair but had escaped.

Jawarski, a former choirboy, had taken a turn from the church and headed into crime early on. As a young man, he became the leader of a group called the Mon Valley Thieves in 1925, when the head honcho, Tony "Torso" Burchanti, was executed. At 5 feet 6 inches and weighing in at 167 pounds, Jawarski was not exactly intimidating, especially as he lay sleeping. But a scar under his chin and on his left cheek, a left middle finger amputated at the middle joint, and a tattoo on the inside of his left forearm gave him a somewhat unsavory appearance.

Now they had Jawarski and some of the other Flatheads, and this time they weren't going to let them go. The suspects were awakened and arrested. The men of course denied all connection with the crime; however, a quantity of dynamite was found concealed under a pile of wood in the woodshed of the farm, and firearms were found in the house. As for money, only $57 was found on Melowski. Stanko, however, had a more telling sign. He had a bankbook on him from the Bank of Detroit that showed a deposit of $5,000. It was recorded just a few days after December 24, 1925, the date when the Flatheads had mortally wounded a payroll guard in another robbery.

As police searched around for more evidence, they noticed a balloon tire on the Ginger Hill Road, 5 miles south of Bentleyville. They then traced a mark on the road caused by running a car on a rim. They followed the rim mark off the road, through a wire fence that had been patched, and into a ravine. There they found an abandoned car with a flat tire. It was a Stearns-Knight, with the license plate number 602-595. The plates were indeed owned by Mr. J. A. Gilmore of Washington Heights, but the car was owned by Dr. Walter Harvey, a Northside physician. The bandits had switched the plates, leaving Gilmore's car in his garage with Harvey's plate, 16-548, on it instead.

By late Saturday night, Brink's was offering $5,000 in reward money for the apprehension and conviction of the other six gang members and 10 percent of any loot that was recovered. Rumors started coming from every direction. State police, private detectives, and officers of boroughs and townships in the Allegheny and Washington counties joined in the chase to find the missing money. More than one hundred volunteers searched the entire farm, near the car, and even in the vicinity of the holdup, thinking they had stashed some of the loot quickly and might come back later. But no money was found.

Meanwhile, the police kept looking for the other Flatheads members. They took pictures to the hospital and showed them to Tarr, the armored car driver who had seen the getaway vehicle. Tarr looked at the police photos and made a positive ID on Dan Rastelli of Meadowlands. Rastelli had been arrested on murder charges in connection to a previous robbery by the Flatheads. He was convicted once but obtained a new trial and was acquitted. Rastelli was found and brought in. All four suspects were convicted.

Since Jawarski was already sentenced to execution, he decided to lead police to $38,000 that had been stashed in milk containers and buried in manure piles on Weckoski's farm. For the next year the field was plowed repeatedly in search of the remaining $66,000, but it was never found. Some speculate that by now it has probably disintegrated, although the case remains open.

As for Jawarski, he was sentenced to die January 21, 1929. But Jawarski didn't go easily. He again escaped from prison, this time with the help of two accomplices, leaving one prison guard dead and two others wounded.

With an epic search that involved more than one hundred police and one hundred detectives, Sam Jawarski, Paul Jawarski's brother and one of the accomplices, was captured in Detroit two months later.

A year later, Paul Jawarski was spotted and caught in a bloody Cleveland, Ohio, restaurant shooting, which left Jawarski paralyzed but not dead. This time while hauling him in, the police took no chances. He was put in a steel-plated car that was armed with guards carrying machine guns, rifles, revolvers, and tear gas. Yet none of this seemed to bother the top Flathead. As Jawarski lay wounded in his stretcher with a slug in his forehead, another in the back of his head, and two more in his shoulder, he looked up at the guards and laughed, "Ain't you glad I got out of jail? Look at the trip you get."

In his final days before the execution, he wrote a letter to his wife in Detroit, with a message for his ten-month-old daughter. "Tell the newspapers that the best thing they can do is warn kids to stay away from things that are bad."

On the last night of his life, Jawarski claimed to have killed John Vasbinder, his other accomplice, saying, "He is running a barber shop 10 miles on the other side of hell." The police didn't buy this story, believing it was just to throw them off his trail.

At 7:02 A.M. on January 21, 1929, Jawarski used his one good arm to help the executioner strap him to the chair. The switch was pulled, ending one of the most violent criminal careers in western Pennsylvania's history.

As for the search for the missing $66,000, the case is still open. If you are ever in the vicinity and need some cash, feel free to search!

The Road to the Future: The Pennsylvania Turnpike

·1940·

Excitement over the opening of a new road might be hard to believe today, but on the night of October 1, 1940, when that seemingly mundane event happened, the evening was filled with a carnival-type atmosphere. But perhaps that is understandable, because this wasn't just a road, it was called a "superhighway," and it was the first of its kind. In fact, it was the prototype of today's interstate highway system. At exactly 12:01 A.M. on a Tuesday, the driving public was allowed access to the newly completed Pennsylvania Turnpike.

Stretching from Middlesex, just west of Harrisburg, 160 miles to Irwin, just east of Pittsburgh, the superhighway boasted unobstructed concrete lanes, no stop signs, no red lights, no railroad crossings, and no intersections. And more interestingly, there wasn't much of a speed limit.

Motorists lined up at all eleven entrance ramps for the delight of being one of the first to ride the "pike" and experience the road of the future. The newspapers had been full of stories about long tunnels that snaked through the Allegheny

Mountains, and many of the drivers were there to check out these tunnels. There were a total of 6.7 miles of tunnels cut through seven different mountains. Inside the tunnels only single lanes accommodated traffic in each direction, but otherwise the highway included two lanes each way from one end to the other.

The road was built as one continuous unit, which required an incredible amount of planning. More than 1,100 engineers were involved to make sure that the thoroughfare never climbed or fell at more than a 3 percent grade; that is, a 3-foot rise or fall for every 100 feet traveled, to avoid dangerous road conditions. More than 300 separate structures were built to accommodate overpasses, underpasses, rivers, streams, and gullies. As well, mountains and hills were moved to create passes that met strict guidelines. Entrance ramps and exit ramps had to meet standards that allowed drivers to get up to speed or slow down with ease.

Enormous thought and argument went into decisions like how wide the lanes would be, how much should be charged in tolls, and how would fees be collected? How many tollbooths would be needed? How would the booths be designed, built, and manned? Where would travelers be able to take a break, get food, or fuel? How could the route be divided to eliminate the fear of high-speed head-on collisions? What method of ventilation would be most effective in the tunnels?

A project of this magnitude could take years to complete even today, despite the fact that we already have the answers to all these questions. Yet this engineering marvel was completed in a mere twenty-five months.

Charles Noble, a design engineer for the Pennsylvania Turnpike Commission, was quoted in the 1940 issue of *Civil Engineering Magazine* as saying, "Unlike the existing highway systems of the United States, in which design standards fluctuate every few miles, depending on the date of construction, the Turnpike will have the same design characteristics throughout its 160 mile length. Every effort has been directed towards securing uniform and consistent operating conditions for the motorist." He went on to say, "In fact, the design was attacked from the viewpoint of motor-car operation and the human frailty of the driver, rather than from that of the difficulty of the terrain and method of construction. This policy of design, based on vehicle operation, is relatively new."

American technology and perseverance paid off. The target opening date was missed only by a few months. The grand opening was not as grand as was originally planned, though; it had been hoped that there would be a ceremony on the Fourth of July with none other than President Franklin Delano Roosevelt in attendance. Inevitable delays prevented this scenario but did little to deter the excitement as the opening at midnight approached.

There were only about twelve hours of official notice before the opening, but word was out that the time was drawing near. Fifty tollbooth collectors, uniformed only in special hats (the full uniforms didn't arrive in time), took their positions as people began to line up early. Attendants at Middlesex, the eastern terminus, turned some 600 people away from 6:00 A.M. to 2:00 P.M. Some of these turn-aways wanted to slip onto the pike early, while others were quite willing to sit in line for a chance to be among the first travelers on this glorious new road. There were reports that one man waited at the Somerset entrance for four days and that a trucker bound for Philadelphia sat in Breezewood starting early Sunday morning. A troupe of ballet dancers traveling across country loitered at the New Stanton Interchange starting on Monday morning. Of course you have to remember that not only was this an exciting new stretch of highway, it was also touted as being a shorter and faster trip than was previously possible.

As midnight approached some people in line started to get antsy. Some tried to cajole the attendants into early ticket purchases. All were turned away with a smile. Cars lined up as reporters interviewed drivers and passengers about their travel plans. The nocturnal backdrop only highlighted the spectacle. Bright blue tollbooths of a very modern style were "lighted like the entrance to a beautiful exposition," reported the *Pittsburgh Sun-Telegraph*.

At last the midnight hour arrived. Like a celebration ringing in the New Year, car and truck horns ushered in the future of motor transportation. Motorists eased into the tollbooths, received stamped yellow tickets, and in some cases were immediately pulled over for official congratulations and interviews. Others sped off to see if all the hype would live up to expectations.

The first driver to enter from the east was Homer D. Romberger. Homer was also present at the groundbreaking ceremony twenty-three months earlier. Shortly behind Mr. Romberger was Bruce Carroll, a native of Ohio returning home.

Over at the western end, the first driver was Carl A. Boe of McKeesport. Mr. Boe got his ticket and was immediately flagged over by two men, Frank Lorey and Dick Gangle, who were attempting to become the first hitchhikers on the new highway. They were successful and will always have their place in history.

Cars and trucks streamed onto the turnpike, and in only a couple of hours, the first travelers started arriving at the opposite ends. People were astonished, since before the pike the average trip from Harrisburg to Pittsburgh took five to six hours. One automobile made the trip to Middlesex from Irwin in two hours and ten minutes. He traveled 160 miles, averaging 74 miles per hour! Other drivers told exciting stories of driving at speeds exceeding 100 miles per hour. And remember, this was a state with a maximum speed limit of 50 miles per hour!

What about the police? What about the speed limits? There was a special police force for the turnpike created by the Pennsylvania State Police. They were trained expressly for this new job and their salaries were to come from the tolls collected.

There had been a lot of discussion about speed limits for the new road, and the general feeling was that speed limits were not necessary. At the last minute, however, Governor Arthur H. James, on advice from an attorney, declared the speed limit for the "super highway" would be just 50 miles per hour. However, no signs were posted and the speed limit was completely ignored by police and motorists alike.

At the end of the first day of operations, thousands of vehicles had traveled for either short jaunts or for long hauls. No serious accidents were reported, and the only complaint lodged by anyone was that the road didn't go far enough. Many people would have liked to see the road extend to Pittsburgh, Philadelphia, or even farther. Of course that day would come.

The rest stops along the highway were fully equipped to provide fuel, food, and emergency services. That was a good thing, since a number of drivers lost track of their gas gauges that first day. The Howard Johnson's restaurants in the rest areas were open twenty-four hours a day and provided full meals as well as their famous ice cream. A steak dinner with three vegetables, soup, salad, bread, butter, drinks, and dessert could be purchased for a whopping 65 cents.

The first week of the turnpike's existence was a smashing success. Word got around quickly, and by October 6 everyone from the Pennsylvania Turnpike Commission was feeling pretty good about the whole operation. That day brought the first "bump in the road," so to speak. It should be noted that the early days of October turn the state of Pennsylvania into a fall foliage wonderland. This Sunday was a beautiful day, and apparently quite a few residents decided this would be a great day to take a Sunday drive on the new superhighway.

Thousands of sightseers poured onto the pike through every interchange. The volume of traffic was so overwhelming that tollbooth personnel ran out of tickets and had to resort to using the tickets meant for light trucks and in some cases handwritten notes. Later in the day came the big problem. Everyone seemed to try to leave at the same time. Traffic was backed up for hours at every exit ramp. Cars were lined up at every fueling station. The Standard Oil Company reported sales of about 50,000 gallons of gasoline. All fifty-nine of the specially trained "Turnpike Troopers" were called into service. It was close to midnight before everything returned to normal, with the final tally showing that more than 27,000 vehicles were processed through the system. Miraculously, there was only one minor accident reported for the entire day.

The doomsayers of the turnpike were predicting traffic volume as low as 715 vehicles per day. In the first fifteen days, the actual count averaged more than 10,000 per day. The Pennsylvania Turnpike was an incredible success from the day it opened. The next time you take a spin on the pike, or any of the other superhighways it spawned, picture those first riders. Imagine the thrill of the wide-open road, and tip your hat to the people who made it possible.

A Shrine for the Lion
· 1942 ·

They had waited four decades for this day. Now hundreds of excited alumni and students were gathered in the appropriately named Happy Valley for the dedication of a shrine to the famous Nittany Lion, a symbol that had come to mean so much to Penn State University. And a symbol that had often raised the question, "What exactly is a Nittany Lion?"

The dedication of the statue took place during homecoming weekend on Saturday, October 24, 1942. The long-awaited ceremony only lasted thirty minutes, during which time the speakers would answer the Nittany Lion question. At exactly 12:50 P.M. the Blue Band started playing. Electricity was in the air. After ten minutes of playing, the music stopped and the ceremonies began. At 1:00, George A. Arisman, the presiding president of the Penn State Alumni Association, rose to give the first speech. He welcomed everyone and then, sensing the crowd's anticipation, turned the podium over to the Class of 1940, the class responsible for voting for the funds to be raised for the statue. Bill Engel, the representative of the Class of 1940 gift committee, began by giving a brief history of how the Nittany name came to be, what it means, and the importance of the statue.

He told how famed Pennsylvania folklorist Henry Shoemaker wrote a book called *The Juniata Memoirs*. The book explains the legend of the creation of Mount Nittany, which was named after Nita-nee. This saintly Indian maiden lived several thousand years ago and was a peace-loving leader who was forced to avenge the attack of her tribe. She won that battle, dismantled her army, and went back to her peaceful ways. Queen Nita-nee was very kind to her tribe, and under her rule there was no nobility: Everyone was equal. Nonetheless, the tribe chose her as their queen.

The queen had requested that upon her death she be buried in the forest under a mound of cedar. At the time of her passing, her burial wishes were respected. That night after the funeral, the earth rumbled and roared.

The next morning, where there was only a small mound the night before, a giant mountain now stood. The mountain broke the breezes from the north, thus protecting the crops and her tribe. Her tribe grew to be prosperous and remained peaceful; knowing their beloved queen forever protected them. The name Nittany lives on as a symbol of peace, prosperity, and protection. And from that time on, the mountains became known as the Nittany Mountains. An excerpt from Shoemaker's book was later edited and published in a 1916 local newspaper and prompted the legend to become part of Penn State's folkloric history. It is from that legend that the school's ordinary mountain lion mascot was later renamed the Nittany Lion and took on all its characteristics—peace, prosperity, and protection.

Engel then concluded his speech, saying, "Now we have completed the shrine, and in such times as these, it is fitting that some object can be looked upon as a symbol of carefree days of pre-game rioting, but also as a focal point for celebrations of victory. The Class of 1940 trusts that the Nittany Lion Shrine will do much toward instilling and maintaining that old Penn State spirit. . . . On behalf of the Class of 1940 and its gift committee . . . I wish to present the Nittany Lion Shrine to the College."

All eyes were upon the sheet-covered shrine. After a dramatic pause, the Class of 1940 lifted the cloth and the limestone shrine was revealed in all its glory. There were oohs and aahs from the crowd and then thunderous applause.

Then the crowd turned silent, as their idol, the man responsible for the legend of the Nittany Lion, was about to speak. The 1907 Penn State graduate and former third baseman, Harrison "Joe" Mason, was a small man, but as one of western Pennsylvania's best semipro baseball players back in 1904, he was more than a minor celebrity.

Mason, dressed in his top coat and hat, stood before the microphone to address the audience and talk about just what happened one bitter cold day in 1904 as his Penn State team, The Penn State Baseball Nine, faced their rival, the Princeton Tigers. "As you students well know, sophomores are generally pretty cocky chaps, and when these two Princeton chaps escorted us into their beautiful gymnasium, they stopped us in front of a splendid mounted figure of a Bengal tiger. One chap spoke up, boasting 'See our emblem, the Princeton Tiger, the fiercest beast of them all.' An idea came to me, and I replied, 'Well up at Penn State we have Mount Nittany right on our campus, there rules the Nittany Mountain Lion, who has never been beaten in a fair fight. So, Princeton Tiger, look out.' . . . Luckily lady luck was with us that afternoon, and our team won."

Joe Mason was indeed lucky, and by the time he graduated, his spur-of-the-moment boast of a nonexistent mascot and name became a reality before he graduated in the spring of 1907.

Up until the Nittany Lion, the school didn't really have a mascot. They had symbols that they adopted from time to time, like that of Coaly the mule, and Andy Lytle, the perennial freshman. The third symbol, an old stuffed lion, was now in a display case in the Old Main Building at Penn State after having toured the country. This lion was the last known mountain lion to roam the forests of Pennsylvania, and it had been shot back in 1856 after an unfortunate encounter with the musket of Samuel Brush. The "Brush lion," as it was originally called, was just gathering dust until one day when the memory of that stuffed 7-foot-9-inch figure flashed into Mason's mind, thus setting the wheels in motion for it to become the permanent school mascot.

This particular lion (also known as the puma, catamount, cougar, or panther) wasn't the strongest or the fastest of its breed. However, this particular lion, immortalized in Penn State University history, was able to do what its brothers and sisters couldn't do: survive, at least in spirit.

While the folklorist Shoemaker couldn't save the lives of the mountain lions, he at least sought to preserve their memory as a matter of state pride. Therefore, he penned another book, *The Pennsylvania Lion or Panther: A narrative of our grandest animal.* Shoemaker had heard stories about how the lion was greatly hated at one time, and he wanted to set the story straight. In his book he wrote, "From the earliest [sic] times the Pennsylvania lion or panther has been unjustly feared. The first Swedish settlers on the Delaware hunted it unmercifully. They could not but believe that an animal which howled so hideously at night must be a destroyer of human life." Town folk reported the lion's cry as bone chilling, a "half-animal, half-human cry" that lasted for well over a minute. Those who heard it never wanted to hear it again. The lion was feared, and so it was hunted into extinction, with the excuse that it was the enemy of poultry.

This "Brush lion" had another thing going for him too: He was the only physical survivor of his species. In 1942, Edward Goldman of the National Museum of Natural History in Washington, D.C., was conducting research on the lions of the eastern mountains. He arranged to borrow *all* the specimens that the Carnegie Museum owned, every skull, tooth, and hide, and loaded them up on a train. While en route to the museum, a freak accident occurred. The car of the train carrying the lion specimens caught on fire, and every inch of them went up in flames. The only example of the lion not consumed by this fire was safe at Penn State. Its survival, according to Duane Schlitter, made the Brush lion "as unique and significant to the history of the Commonwealth as is William Penn's original deed to Penn's Forest." (As a side note: From that day forward no museum ever shipped an entire collection of any species again.)

Mason concluded his speech, "We see before us the real Nittany Mountain Lion—alert, resourceful, unafraid, unconquerable, an inspiration to every loyal son and daughter of Old Penn State for generations to come." And with that, the man whose improvisational boast was responsible for it all, sat down humbly to thunderous applause.

At 1:16 P.M. Bernard Plesser, '43, president of the athletic association, expressed his appreciation and talked about the statue's creator, a gifted German sculptor named Heinz Warneke. Warneke who was renowned for his extraordinary sculptures of animals. He was commissioned in the summer of 1941 and finished the sculpture in just four months. Warneke was paid a sum of $5,375 for his work. The entire shrine was completed in a little over a year, in time for the first home football game with Bucknell on October 3, 1942.

Plesser closed the ceremony by saying, "The Nittany Lion is here. Here . . . is a legend and a tradition to which we can pledge our allegiance, a legend which we can cherish dear, and a legend which we call, 'The Symbol of our Best.'"

The ceremony closed at 1:26 with the Blue Band playing the school theme song, "The Nittany Lion." The crowd dispersed, and people patted the lion on the head for good luck as they passed.

The statue of the Nittany Lion still stands today on Penn State campus, as does the original stuffed Nittany. They are never lonely. People passing by the stuffed lion salute, and as for the statue, the sculptor, Warneke, has visited his work three times to do repairs. Various fraternities of the college follow a time-honored tradition of guarding the lion to prevent graffiti and damage. Cats, dogs, goats, beauty queens, and campus leaders and heroes have posed with the statue.

Finally, let's not forget those who bring the lion to life, those highly trained gymnasts who wear the Nittany Lion mascot suit. Over the years each one of them has understood the significance of this majestic creature. They consider it "the most honorable position that can be bestowed upon a Penn State student." Now that's a statement that can make even a stone lion roar.

The Steagles:
A One-Year Wonder
in the World of
Professional Football
· 1943 ·

How about a little world-class football trivia? Which National League Football team holds the all-time record for having the most fumbles in a single game? The answer is the Steagles, of course. What the heck is a Steagle? For the answer to that question, we have to travel back in time, all the way back to 1943.

At that time, the country was embroiled in World War II, and most able-bodied men were away fighting in the war. The National Football League was still in its adolescence, and the leaders of the league had some tough decisions to make. First and foremost was the question of whether the season should simply be cancelled in light of the war. President Franklin Delano Roosevelt stepped into the fray with his opinion, stating he thought that the professional football season should go on because it would be good for the country's morale.

League officials knew it would be difficult to field qualified players in the games, and the league was hampered by new restrictions, including a travel restriction that called for the teams to cut travel by 37 percent in order to conserve for the war effort. This meant schedules had to be reconfigured, and all team rosters were reduced from thirty-three players to twenty-eight. This reduction would reduce travel costs because with fewer players, the entire team could fit on one bus. Another complication was the loss of the Cleveland Rams franchise, who couldn't assemble a full team that year due to all the complications. This left the league unbalanced. Another team would have to be cut, but which one?

At the urging of NFL Commissioner Elmer Layden, the co-owners of the Pittsburgh Steelers, Art Rooney Sr. and Bert Bell, worked out a deal with Philadelphia Eagles owner Alexis Thompson. To ensure the survival of both teams, they decided to combine forces and form a single Pennsylvania team. This team was known by different names, including the Phil-Pitt Eagles-Steelers, but over time they came to be known simply as the Pennsylvania Steagles.

Finding a new name was just one of many confusing issues. Who would be the coach? The teams had very capable coaches in Walt Kiesling of the Pittsburgh franchise and Earl "Greasy" Neale of Philadelphia. The solution to this issue was decided by the King Solomon method: The coaching duties would be split between the two men right down the middle.

Next came some delicate massaging of the roster. With so many players gone to war, it fell to the team owners to scrounge among the leftovers. Older players were called out of retirement, and players who would not normally have made the cut were now starters. Some players invited to play even had physical irregularities that previously kept them out of the league entirely. Another problem for the coaches was that, after the merging of the teams, some positions had more than one capable player while other positions were left completely vacant. There was nothing to do but retrain some team members to play unfamiliar positions.

The news of all this reshuffling didn't filter down to the players like it would today, when we can just "reach out and touch someone." The rookie tackle Bucko Kilroy came to the Eagles from Philadelphia's North Catholic High School by way of Temple University. In a recent interview, Kilroy revealed that he learned of the new team designation only after his arrival in camp. "We didn't know," said Kilroy. "I was in the service [the Merchant Marines] and I could only play part time." Scheduling conflicts didn't keep him out of the games, though: Kilroy managed to be a soldier and a Steagle, too.

Like Kilroy, Al Wistert showed up at his very first NFL training camp that year thinking he was a member of the Philadelphia Eagles. He had never heard anything about the merger, and it wasn't until the end of his first practice session that he found out he wasn't an Eagle but rather a Steagle. Wistert had been a big-shot college star at the University of Michigan. He was an All-American and voted as the most valuable player by his college teammates. When he negotiated his professional contract with the Eagles agent, he demanded the outrageous sum of $4,500 per year in salary. This struck the agent as a very funny proposition. Of course, in today's market that is approximately how much the average player makes per minute of a single game. A compromise was reached at $3,700, but word got back to some of the veteran players about the upstart rookie's ridiculous demand. According to Wistert this made for a very difficult training camp as the older players showed their disapproval. Even with his outrageous salary, Wistert didn't get a starting place on the team. Steelers veteran Ted Doyle played the same position and beat him out for the top spot, despite the fact that he was paid a lot less.

Personnel problems were worked out on the practice field, but the playing field itself became an issue. Where would the team play its home games? Luckily, the schedule the league produced solved that problem. Home games against teams west of

Pennsylvania were played primarily at Pittsburgh's Forbes Field, while teams from the east played in Philadelphia's Shibe Park. This had the added benefit of helping the war effort by reducing travel and leaving more resources available for the war.

All of these problems were met and solved before the Steagles played a single down. Neither of these two teams separately were what you would call a powerhouse in the NFL. The Eagles had never even had a winning season, meaning that they never won more games in a year than they lost. The Steelers' record was better by exactly one season: The previous year had been Pittsburgh's first and only winning season.

Despite these poor showings in the past, the Steagles turned out to be a pretty darn good team. They won their first two games, both played in Philadelphia's Shibe Park, against the Brooklyn Dodgers and the New York Giants. They lost their next two games, first to the Chicago Bears, then in a rematch with the Giants in New York.

In their next game the national champion Washington Redskins rode into Philly only to be turned away with an embarrassing fourteen to fourteen tie. There were no sudden-death playoffs in those days and games regularly ended in a tie. This was particularly embarrassing due to the fact that the Redskins were led by the famous Hall of Fame quarterback "Slinging" Sammy Baugh. On October 31 the Chicago Cardinals got a Halloween scare when they came to Pittsburgh for the first Steagle game to be played at Forbes Field. The Cardinals got smashed like a leftover pumpkin in a thirty-four to thirteen loss.

A second visit with the Dodgers in Brooklyn wasn't as satisfying as the first. The Steagles were unable to "dodge" a loss on Brooklyn's home turf. The Detroit Lions roared into Pittsburgh on November 21, but the steady Steagles tamed the Lions and eked out a one-point victory with the final score of thirty-five to thirty-four. A trip south to the nation's capital brought the Pennsylvanians face to face with the mighty Redskins again. This time there was no doubt, as the visiting Steagles shot down the Redskins by the respectable margin of twenty-seven to fourteen.

In the final game of their existence, the Steagles fell to the Green Bay Packers in Philadelphia in a high-scoring shootout that finished with the hybrid Pennsylvania team on the short end of a thirty-eight to twenty-eight score. The now-beloved Steagles completed their one and only season with a winning record of five wins, four losses, and one tie.

It had been an exciting season with many high points. Steagles star running back Jack Hinkle finished the season with more rushing yards than any other player in the league. Tony Bova was the team's leading receiver with seventeen catches, which was an incredible performance considering that Tony was completely blind in one eye and only had partial vision in the other. Hall of Fame receiver Bill Hewitt had come out of a four-year retirement to help the team. He only caught two passes all year and immediately retired after the season, this time for good.

And yes, the Steagles still are in the record books. The Pennsylvania Steagles set the record for the most fumbles in a single game with a total of ten. Certainly this is not a record to be proud of, but it is one that still stands to this day. Other teams have matched the record; however, no one seems to be willing to take it away. And even though it may be hard to believe, the game with the ten fumbles was against the New York Giants, and the Steagles still won the game.

So in the final analysis, the Steagle is an eagle made of steel, and as it turns out this "metal bird" really could fly.

The Toy That Walked into Fame
·1945·

It would be nice to come up with a million-dollar invention. What's even nicer is if that million-dollar invention literally walks into your life. Of course all that one needs is the insight to spot it. And luckily for Richard James, a naval engineer earning $50 a week at the Cramp Shipyard in Philadelphia in 1943, he had both the opportunity and the insight.

James was working at his desk one afternoon, trying to develop a meter that would monitor the horsepower on naval ships. One of the components of this meter was a torsion spring; technically, it was a rather boring-looking spring because it had zero compression and zero tension. As he was fidgeting around with one spring, another torsion spring just like it fell off a shelf.

As any normal person would do, he stopped what he was doing to see what fell. But this spring did not just fall dead to the ground; rather this spring had a little two-step of its own. The spring literally leapt off the shelf, onto his desk, walked across a row of books, and then bounced to the floor. Those who are easily spooked would have thought it a poltergeist. But for Richard, the proverbial lightbulb went off in his head.

That night he rushed home to his wife Betty and said, "I think we got something here." He took the average-looking spring, placed it on the steps in his home, and watched it walk down the stairs. Betty just looked at her husband and asked, "What is it?" James smiled and said, "Maybe we can make a toy out of this." Within minutes, their one-year-old son Tommy was playing with it. He was fascinated by the way it moved. Betty smiled at her husband. "Whatever you want to do with it, you have my backing 100 percent." She knew genius when she saw it. Besides, both men in her life seemed to be thrilled with it.

For the next two years, Richard kept his day job and experimented with torsion springs whenever he got the chance. He had to create a spring that would walk down stairs each and every time. Finally in 1945, after much trial and error, and much field testing on the part of his wife and their growing family, he felt he had the perfect toy.

Being novices in business, they weren't sure exactly what to do next, but they decided they should form a company, give their toy a name, and obtain a patent. The first part was easy; they called themselves James Industries. Then Betty looked through the dictionary for some ideas for the toy's name. Finally she found it, the perfect word. It was Swedish, and it perfectly described their average-looking spring: *slinky*. According to the dictionary it meant "stealthy, sleek, and sinuous." Not to mention that the word *slinky* had a catchy sound to it. So Slinky it was. Next, they did what most first-time inventors who are low on cash do: They borrowed money. With their borrowed $500 they found a company to manufacture the first several hundred springs. But now they were stumped, as Betty said: "We were as green as apples; once we had the Slinkys made up we didn't have the slightest idea what to do with them." They knew they couldn't just stick them on shelves in the stores and hope for the best.

Then one November day, they decided to go to Gimbel's, one of the biggest stores in downtown Philadelphia. Betty and Richard met with the toy buyer in the store and showed him the Slinky. The buyer was interested, but he wasn't sure it would sell. Still, he was willing to give them a try. He gave the

Jameses a tiny little corner in the toy department to display the Slinky for the 1945 Christmas season. They would have those two months to prove themselves. It was a season that would make or break them.

That same evening, an eager Richard came back to the store with 400 Slinkys in hand and was ready to give it his best shot, even though it was hailing and snowing outside. Knowing that they had worked long and hard on this project and that the weather would probably keep most people away, Betty wanted to tip the scale in their favor. She was worried about Richard's morale if not one of them sold. So, she arranged for one of her friends to go by Richard's table and buy the first Slinky, just to get the ball rolling, or in this case the spring bouncing.

That evening as the ringer and Betty walked through the store, they noticed an eerie feeling. The store was dead; there was absolutely nothing going on. Betty's heart sank as she walked toward the toy department. Two years of experimenting and endless hours were at stake. Betty said, turning to her friend, "At least Richard will make one sale tonight."

As they got closer to the toy department, they started to hear a strange noise. It sounded like a muffled roar. As they turned the corner into the toy department, they saw a large crowd gathered. People where shouting, pushing, and holding dollar bills over their heads. Betty and her friend made their way closer. It was Richard. He was selling the Slinkys as fast as he could take the customers' money. Betty worked her way to the small counter and happily helped her husband with the sales. She turned to her husband and asked, "What happened?" He explained that he began by demonstrating the Slinky. Then customer after customer started playing with it, and soon the toys were selling themselves. They sold out their entire 400 Slinkys on that snow-covered night in just ninety minutes! The toy buyer looked on from the corner with a smile. He knew he had a winner.

The next day they took their entire profits and ordered 1,000 Slinkys to be made by the manufacturer. And this is how they built their business. Sell, buy, sell. Originally there was no box for the toy, but Betty's job was to put a rolled up yellow sheet of instructions into one of the coils of each Slinky. They ran their business from the dining room of their house.

The Jameses were working night and day to keep up with the demand. At night they were packing instructions into the Slinkys and doing the paperwork, while during the day they were personally going from store to store demonstrating the product. But they still had a cash flow problem. They didn't have the money to place advance orders, so they had to wait to sell out before they could place the next order. Retailers co-operated with them because they saw that this toy could make their holiday season. No one wanted to be without a Slinky in December of 1945—no one, not even the manufacturer, and that's where Betty and Richard ran into their first big problem. The manufacturer of the springs turned to them in the middle of December and said, "We're going to make 'em for ourselves and sell 'em." Richard told the manufacturer that they couldn't do that, that James Industries had a patent on the Slinky. The manufacturer just laughed and began to produce the Slinky on his own.

James Industries quickly filed a lawsuit, and then Richard, being the engineer that he was, quickly began inventing his own Slinky-producing machine in his father's small pattern shop in Germantown, Pennsylvania. What looked like bad luck turned out to be the best thing for them. Richard's machine produced the 80-foot Slinkys faster and more efficiently than the underhanded manufacturer could, whether he was doing it legally or illegally. That first season they did so well that Richard quit his job and produced Slinkys full time.

Meanwhile Betty wore quite a few hats. She would go to the shop each evening, pack the day's production of Slinkys, handle all the accounting and paperwork, then go home and take care of her two children (and she was expecting their third child, as well). By the end of their two-month trial Christmas season, they proved to Gimbel and the rest of the world that two novices could become an overnight sensation. Plus, they had won their lawsuit. One might expect the next words to be "and they lived happily ever after." Not so.

For the next few years the Slinky grew despite Richard and Betty's mistakes along the way. For more than ten years, the couple worked side by side. Then Richard suddenly changed. At first he became a partier and womanizer. Then, just as suddenly, he had a complete change of heart and joined a religious cult, giving nearly all the company profits to the cult leaders. In addition, he inserted religious messages into every Slinky package, berating customers and badmouthing other religions. Sales plummeted as he alienated customers and lost major accounts. Repeatedly Betty would order the messages taken out, and Richard would order them put back in. The company was nearing bankruptcy, with only four employees remaining of the 125 in their heyday. Total annual revenue stood at a mere $121,000.

Then on February 22, 1959, at 11:00 P.M., a day Betty will always remember, Richard came home from one of his religious cult meetings and announced he was going to become a full-time Christian and work in Bolivia. He said he no longer cared about material wealth. He turned to Betty, "Are you going to sell the company or run it?" Without hesitation Betty, having known nothing else for years, said, "Run it." And run it she did.

With Richard in Bolivia, Betty raised their six kids and ran the company that she once helped start. With hard work, and patient retailers, she turned the business around and made it into the multimillion-dollar business it is today. The company became a major force, and she ran it with the help of her oldest son Tom, one of the first field-testers. The once-naive Betty changed the packaging, added colored and animal Slinkys to the line, replaced the original Slinky material of blue-black

Swedish steel with the now famous silver-colored American metal, and realized the value in advertising.

The little spring that walked into their lives was used in the first American satellite in space; used by executives to relieve tension; studied in college physics classes; used as a tool by physical therapists; was an inspiration for engineers in building a coil antenna used by the military; and was used by the Philadelphia Phillies to improve finger dexterity (and that was the year they went on to win the pennant!).

As for the creators, Richard James died of a heart attack in Bolivia in 1974. The Slinky brand was sold in 1998 to Poof Toys. And Betty James, grandmother and entrepreneur, was inducted into the Toy Industry Hall of Fame in 2001.

The Death Fog
· 1948 ·

Before there was an Environmental
Protection Agency, before there was an Earth Day,
before Rachel Carson wrote *Silent Spring,*
there was Donora.

—Michael McCabe,
U.S. Environmental Protection Agency

Donora is a small industrial river town south of Pittsburgh, located on the western bank of the Monongahela River. The town is nicknamed the Horseshoe Bottom, because the river curves in a horseshoe shape at the bottom of the town. It is surrounded by hills that rise about 400 feet from the bottom of the river and are about a mile apart, in essence leaving the town in a valley. Cobblestone streets snake up and down the hills, which are so steep that in some places they require stairs instead of sidewalks. In the early 1700s grain flourished in this fertile valley, which attracted many people to the area.

By 1948, 14,000 people lived in Donora and many thousands more lived in the surrounding area. Industry moved into the valley in a big way, mainly because Donora was an anti-union town. Union Steel Company had a mill, and Carnegie Steel Company had two blast furnaces, twelve open-hearth furnaces, and a 40-foot mill. Both Matthew Woven Wire Fence Company and Donora Zinc Works had mills. That was a lot of mills for one little valley, but the people of Donora didn't mind because mills meant work and work meant money.

All these mills produced smoke, smoke that lingered high above the town until it eventually blew away. But to the Donorans the smoke was beautiful, and often on summer nights they would sit out on their porches and watch the sky light up for miles with the glowing fiery dust and gases from the furnaces, which produced gorgeous sunsets. No one had a clue then about pollution, or that this smoke was harmful.

But this all changed during the week of October 23, 1948, when an atmospheric phenomenon known as an inversion came to town. An inversion exists when a warm air mass traps cold air near the ground. The problem with an inversion in an area that is emitting pollution is that the inversion not only traps air but everything that is in the air as well.

To the people of Donora, this inversion just meant a persistent dense fog that hung suspended above the town. By the morning of October 26, all the gases from Donora's mills, furnaces, and stoves that normally floated away to annoy other towns became so intense that they slowly began to choke the townspeople.

At first, the cars and trucks crept along the highway, blinded by the fog that consisted of coal, coke, metal fumes and fluoride. It was broad daylight and the motorists were driving with their headlights on to try to see the other cars. By mid-afternoon it got so bad that traffic came to a complete standstill because drivers could not even see the street. One young steelworker, Vince Graziano, who was in Donora that day, commented, "I could not even see my hand at the end of my arm. I actually could not find my way home. I got lost that day." The strange thing was that the fog did not alarm the people of Donora. They figured it would just go away as suddenly as it came. Some residents had complained before to city officials that the fumes "ate the paint off of houses," but since nothing was done, they had learned to live with it. Besides, there had been fog trapped in the valley before, and the towns-people did enjoy the astonishingly beautiful sunsets.

One of the town's leading attorneys and a resident of fifty years, Arnold Hirsh, says he remembers watching the smog gather on the main streets through his office window. "The air looked yellow, never like that before. Nothing moved." He walked outside and stood at the corner of McKean and Seventh Street and looked towards the river. He could barely make out the railroad tracks. He walked closer to get a better look. Right there on the tracks was a coal-burning engine, just puffing black smoke into the air. The billowing smoke went up about 6 feet and then stopped cold. "It just hung there, with no place to go, in air that did not move." It was a creepy feeling even for that World War II veteran, who had seen a lot of things.

The next day the fog was still there, yet the people of Donora were still not overly concerned. It was Friday afternoon and the annual Halloween parade was planned. Since this was an annual community event, the whole town turned out. To some the spooky haze that hung over the town just added to the ambience. Of course spectators could barely see their own feet, much less the parade of masqueraded children as they ap-peared and disappeared in the mysterious mist.

On Saturday morning the townspeople were again out in numbers; these hardy folks simply refused to let the fog stop any of their planned festivities. This time the event was the football game between Donora and Monongahela High School. Spectators watched the game as best they could but they often lost sight of the ball as it disappeared into the fog. The refer-ees would blow their whistles, and the crowd would cheer as a matter of instinct.

Then it happened. The first sign of danger hit the towns-people. Over the loudspeaker, right in the middle of the game, a name was called out. "Stanley Sawa. Stanley Sawa. Go home. Go home now." The crowd was in shock. Stanley was Donora's star tight end. Why was he being ordered home?

Some spectators thought it was a Halloween prank being pulled by the opposing team. But the announcement went out again. "Stanley Sawa. Go home now."

With helmet in hand Stanley raced off the field and in full uniform ran home. When he got there a neighbor was in the house. "What's the matter? Why was I called home?" The neighbor told him that his dad, who had been working at the mill, came home feeling a little dizzy. Stanley's eyes searched the house. "I'm afraid he's dead, Stanley," said the neighbor.

By the time the rest of the fans left the football field, nine more people had died. This was the fourth day of the inversion. The fumes, which were stagnant at street level, were taking no prisoners.

There were eight doctors in the town of Donora, and all used to make regular house calls. But this time, no doctors would come. They were too weak to make the rounds. As one doctor said to anyone who called, "The whole town is sick. Even healthy fellas are dropping. Get the hell out of town!"

Some families drove into the Allegheny Mountains to get away. Those who made it to Palmer Park, a park which sat up on the hill, started to recover right away. Firemen went door to door, giving whiffs of oxygen from their tanks to those who were too sick or stranded to make it out of town.

By the fifth day, twenty more residents had died. The local funeral home had run out of caskets, and the basement of the community center became a temporary morgue. Seven thousand people—half of the town's population—had been sick or hospitalized. Most were having difficulty breathing. Some were nauseous, some had severe sore throats, some had eyes and noses that were swollen and irritated. The very factories that employed the townspeople were killing them.

Not taking blame, but in the interest of "precaution," all the factories closed down, except for the zinc furnaces (once they are cooled they can never be restarted). As one resident observed, "When the smelting plant closed briefly after the cri-sis you could breathe normally again."

The Donora Death Fog, as it became known, shocked the nation when Walter Winchell did a report on it on the evening news. "Good evening, America! The small working town of Donora, Pennsylvania, is in mourning as they recover from a catastrophe. People dropped dead from a thick killer fog that sickened much of the town. Folks are investigating what has hit the area." Not one death certificate related to this tragedy listed pollution as cause of death. Instead "asthma attack," "Chronic heart disease," and "tuberculosis" were listed. Over the course of the next month, fifty more people died from "lingering health damage." This catastrophe marked a turning point in the government's attitude toward clean air.

The incident was investigated by the Pennsylvania De-partment of Health, United Steelworkers, Donora's Borough Council, and the U.S. Public Health Service. Unfortunately the results were inconclusive, stating that "The studies of Donora Smog did not fix blame and could not document levels of pollution beyond workplace limits set at the time." In other words, they weren't ready to admit that smog coming from the factories could have caused those deaths. But as one local newspaper, the *Monessen Daily Independent,* put it, "Damage from the air pollution from Zinc Works was something no sci-entific investigation is necessary to prove. All you need is a pair of reasonably good eyes."

Despite numerous requests by citizens and health care professionals for answers, the facts and statistics that were com-piled by the investigating agencies were kept hidden for years. After doing extensive research on the disaster site, Philip Sadtler, the nation's leading expert on fluorine pollution and a top industrial chemical consultant, said, "the U.S. Steel com-pany conspired with the U.S. Public Health Service (PHS) to cover up the role that fluoride played in this tragedy." Why would they do such a thing? Because "the cost of a national flu-oride cleanup would have been in the billions." Keeping the true cause of the deaths a secret was vital. "It would have com-plicated things enormously for them if the public had been alerted to the (dangers of) fluoride." In plain language, Sadtler said, "It was murder."

Eventually the public demanded the company records of U.S. Steel, but unfortunately every single record in the Public Health Service archives was "destroyed" in a mysterious fire. And those that were the company property of U.S. Steel were closed to reporters, researchers, and outside investigators. A class action lawsuit was brought on by Donora victim families and each case was later settled out of court with the big com-panies.

Even without the solid proof, the Donora Disaster scared enough people in important places to become the catalyst for the federal government's first real effort in 1955 at regulating air pollution. The regulation eventually lead to the Clean Air Act of 1970, which forced states to come up with plans for reduc-ing pollution to meet federal standards. The Donora incident also sparked the creation of the Environmental Protection Agency.

Although our air today is not 100 percent clean, we are in a lot better shape today than in the past. We have removed 98 percent of the lead from the air, 41 percent of sulfur dioxide, 28 percent of the carbon monoxide, and 25 percent of the smog mess we call ozone. The bottom line is we need breath-able air, a fact that anyone in Donora who lived through that horrible time will gladly tell you.

The Homer by the Fielder

· 1960 ·

Bill Mazeroski hit a one-of-a-kind home run on October 13, 1960, in old Forbes Field in Pittsburgh, Pennsylvania. Never before in the history of professional baseball had a World Series ended with a walk-off home run. The mighty New York Yankees were knocked off their pedestal by the scrappy Pittsburgh Pirates.

It doesn't seem possible that the Pirates won the series, looking at the lopsided statistics, which show that the Yankees should have walked away with it. Yankee sluggers out-hit the Pirates by a margin of ninety-one to sixty through the seven-game series, and the New Yorkers scored a total of twenty-eight more runs. The Pirates were out-homered ten to four and lost the battle on the pitcher's mound by a substantial number as well. New York pitchers had an ERA (earned run average per nine innings) that was close to half the Pittsburgh number. Ask any baseball manager to take those kinds of numbers in a World Series, and I guarantee he'll jump at the chance. But a fast check of the math shows that it is not desirable to win three baseball games by what could only be called landslides while losing four games by a mere run or two.

A quick summary of the series shows that the Pittsburgh Pirates snuck by New York in the first game with a score of six to four. Mazeroski played a significant role in this game by hitting the go-ahead home run in front of the home-field fans. The next two games, one in Pittsburgh and one in New York, were both blowouts in favor of the Mickey Mantle–led Yankees. The scores were sixteen to three and ten to zero, respectively, with Whitey Ford pitching the shutout in the Bronx.

Game Four, also played at Yankee stadium, was a classic pitcher's duel featuring two of baseball's best pitchers. Pittsburgh's Vernon Law was just a little stingier than New York's Ralph Terry, allowing fewer Yankees to round the bases. Law and the Pirates came away with a series-tying three to two win. Vernon Law won that game almost by himself. In addition to a spectacular pitching display, he also provided the Pirates' first run by hitting a double in the fifth inning and later coming around to score the deciding run.

The fifth meeting of these champions rested in the hands of Bucs (another name for a Pirate and short for Buccaneer) pitcher Harvey Haddix. Harvey got off to a rocky start by giving up two runs in the first three innings. He buckled down, and with help from Pirate reliever Elroy Face, held the dangerous Yankee bats in check for the remainder of the game. The five to two victory gave Pittsburgh a three to two edge as the action left Yankee Stadium and moved back to western Pennsylvania.

Pittsburgh fans were excited to close out the series as Game Six got underway. Whitey Ford had other plans and showed his prowess by tossing another shutout. The Yankees demolished the Pirates twelve to zero and this set the stage for one of the most improbable final games in World Series history.

Thursday, October 13, 1960, arrived with all the excitement of a Game Seven in any World Series. Add to the mix the fantastic lineup of future Hall of Fame players that the fans were watching: Mickey Mantle, Roger Maris, Yogi Berra, and Whitey Ford for the Yankees, and Roberto Clemente, Willie Stargell, Vernon Law, and Manny Sanguillen for the Pirates. The two great teams had played their hearts out for an entire base-ball season and it all came down to one game. Win and you are champions, lose and you go home.

Forbes Field, located on Pittsburgh's west side was filled to capacity and the home crowd got plenty of reasons to cheer as the Pirates jumped to an early four to zero lead. But no one was surprised as the Bronx Bombers slowly worked their way back into the game. Mantle, Berra, and Bill Skowron provided impor-tant offensive plays, and by the eighth inning the powerful Yan-kee team maneuvered into the lead by a score of seven to four.

Gino Cimoli got things started in the bottom of the eighth for Pittsburgh with a pinch hit single. Then Bill Virdon hit a sharp grounder toward Yankee shortstop Tony Kubek. A per-fect example of the expression "It all depends on which way the ball bounces," this ball took a bad hop for New York, jump-ing up and catching Tony right in the throat. What should have been a momentum-shifting double play ended up with both Pirates safe and an injured Kubek out of the game. Dick Groat knocked another single next and the Yankee lead was cut to just two runs. The great Roberto Clemente beat out an infield hit to keep the rally alive and push in another run. With only a one-run lead and runners on first and third, Hal Smith stepped up to the plate and sent daggers through the hearts of Yankee fans everywhere by belting a three-run homer over the left-field fence. Pandemonium broke out in Pittsburgh as their Pirates blasted into a nine to seven lead.

By now one can see why this game is considered one of the most dramatic in World Series history. Home runs, injuries, and lead changes make for exciting baseball, but there was an-other inning to play and, as Yogi Berra once said, "It ain't over till it's over."

Pirates manager Danny Murtaugh sent eighteen-game winner Bob Friend to the mound to safeguard the two-run advantage. Two Yankees, Bobby Richardson and pinch hitter Dale Long, reacted in a most un"Friend"ly manner. Both ended up on base with singles and Murtaugh swiftly replaced Friend with Harvey Haddix. The heart of the Yankee batting order paced in the dugout, just waiting for a chance to shine. Haddix got Roger Maris to foul out, but Mantle whacked a vital single that scored Richardson and moved Long to third. That brought up the tenacious Yogi Berra. Yogi hit a soft grounder to Pirate first baseman Rocky Nelson, who stepped on first for the second out. A game filled with memorable moments was about to add another. Mickey Mantle realized he was a sure out at second so he did the only thing possible: In true all-star style he headed back to first base, somehow eluding Rocky's tag. If Mantle were tagged out that would end the series. Instead the distraction allowed Long to score from third. The Yankees stayed alive to see the bottom of the ninth with the score tied at nine runs apiece.

Bill Mazeroski strode to the plate to start the bottom of the ninth facing Ralph Terry, who had been brought in to finish the last out of the eighth. With a count of one ball and no strikes, Terry served up the pitch that Maz and Pirates fans everywhere will remember as long as they live. The Pittsburgh second baseman, famed for his defensive work, drove the ball over the left-field fence. The crowd at Forbes Field went wild. The Yankees and their fans were dismayed. New York dominated the series, but that was not enough.

"Losing the 1960 series was the biggest disappointment of my career," said Mickey Mantle. "I don't know what the pitch was (to Mazeroski in Game Seven). All I know is it was the wrong one," exclaimed Ralph Terry.

Is it possible that this was the greatest game played in World Series history? Certainly many people have varying opinions about that, but no one can argue that it was one of the best. To this day no other World Series has ended with a home run in the bottom half of the ninth inning of the seventh game.

Bill Mazeroski has a lot to be proud of in his illustrious career. He holds the major league records for most career double plays, most double plays in a single season, and nine seasons leading the national league in assists. He was a six-time All-star and an eight-time Gold Glove winner. Nonetheless, a great deal of controversy surrounded his possible induction into the Hall of Fame. It seems that some people didn't think he had enough offensive ability to earn the honor. However, many others believe his defensive skills were enough on their own; with the addition of the important offense that he did contribute to the game, you have a no-brainer.

Bill Mazeroski was elected into the Baseball Hall of Fame in Cooperstown, New York, in 2001 by the veterans committee. No one in Pittsburgh will ever forget the crack of Mazeroski's bat that dashed the dreams of the mighty New York Yankees.

Roswell Comes to Pennsylvania
· 1965 ·

On the cold evening of December 9, 1965, at around 4:45 P.M., thousands of people from Michigan, Ohio, Pennsylvania, and parts of Canada saw a bright, fiery object soar through the sky above the Great Lakes, an object they claimed looked like a plane plummeting to the earth. In its wake it left a smoky trail that lingered at least twenty minutes. As the object made a sudden turn just over Pittsburgh, the police, the media, and the Allegheny County Observatory were flooded with people calling to find out what was happening. Local fire departments were called to the scene in towns throughout the country to investigate reports of flaming fragments falling from the sky.

Meanwhile, unaware of all the commotion, a seven-year-old boy and his sister were playing outside their house in Kecksburg, a small town in southwestern Pennsylvania, just 40 miles southeast of Pittsburgh. Suddenly the boy noticed a bright light in the sky. He ran inside the house and yelled, "Mommy, a star is on fire!" His mother, Frances Kalp, came outside and said she noticed a "column of blue smoke rising through the trees from the woods about a mile away where the object landed, and another brilliant object hanging above the tree line and to the left of the smoke column." She and her children went into the woods directly behind their home to investigate. When they were about half a mile from the smoking object, they suddenly stopped. Peering through the darkness, they saw an odd craft resembling a four-pointed star. The scene felt creepy to Frances, and she didn't want to put her kids in harm's way, so she turned her kids around and they all headed home. For some reason, she decided that, instead of calling the police, she would phone WHJB, the local radio station in nearby Greensburg, to report what she had seen. John Murphy, the news director of the station, answered her call. After listening to her story, he decided to call the Pennsylvania State Police Department. The police department in turn called Mrs. Kalp and arranged to meet with her near the site. Meanwhile Murphy decided he needed to get an interview with this woman himself, and while he was at it, take a peek at this thing she claimed to have seen.

Murphy arrived shortly after the police had taken an official report from Mrs. Kalp. He interviewed the woman and her two kids while the police were in the woods searching for the downed object. Murphy then took a quick look around without anyone noticing and decided to wait for the return of the searchers. When the searchers returned, Murphy was unable to get any clear answers from the two policemen who were leading the search, Carl Metz and Paul Shipco. They told him that the military was being called in to handle the case.

Determined to get answers, Murphy called his contact, Captain Joseph Dussia, at the police station headquarters in Greensburg to find out what the searchers found. He was told by the captain to come down to the police station to hear the "official statement" that was about to be delivered. In the few minutes it took him to get to the station, the military had already arrived there in force. After a few hushed conversations, an official announcement was made: "The Pennsylvania State Police have made a thorough search of the woods. We are convinced that there is nothing whatsoever in the woods."

Murphy figured that some kind of cover-up was going on, so he phoned in a quick "official" report to his radio station and decided to hang around the police station to see what else he could find out.

His persistence paid off. He overheard policemen who were at the scene mention a "pulsating blue light" in the forest. The captain then told Murphy that Officer Metz and the military were going back into the woods and that Murphy could go along for the ride. He was thrilled to be included on the second search but also dubious about what the captain told him. Why would the police and military go back to the woods if they said nothing was there? Were they planning to reexamine the nothingness? Murphy's bubble was soon burst when they arrived at the scene. Murphy wasn't allowed to enter the woods. He watched as the military sealed off the area, banning all civilians from entering the woods and the immediate area. Those nosy civilians that had wandered into the woods prior to the military getting there were quietly whisked away and questioned. With the banning of the area, curiosity rose to an all-time high. Television and newspaper reporters flocked to the site, and people came in droves, trying to see what they believed was going to be some kind of historic event.

Theories were buzzing around the town. Was it a meteor? A fragment of a comet? A downed plane? An alien spacecraft? By the end of the day, another statement was released, this time by the Air Force, stating that "a meteorite was responsible for the report of a glowing craft, and the subsequent crash in the woods." The media reported this statement, and it seemed that almost everyone accepted this explanation.

By the next morning the town of Kecksburg was once again quiet, the military forces had left, and the whole thing seemed as if it never happened. However, not everyone was willing to accept the government's explanation. Several researchers investigated for years on their own, interviewing eye witnesses and gathering information. Somehow the research made it to the media, and years later, the town of Kecksburg became a hotbed of controversy in 1990 when the television show *Unsolved Mysteries* decided to air a segment on the Sci-Fi Channel about what happened in Kecksburg that night. The segment was titled, "The New Roswell: Kecksburg Exposed." After years of production and controversy, it finally aired on Friday, October 24, 2003.

According to *Unsolved Mysteries,* its researchers and other experts uncovered information that was not initially reported, much of which appears to have been covered up by the government. The show reported that some local citizens who were closer to the action in Kecksburg decided to investigate the object on their own before calling in any state officials. These people reported a different experience than those who viewed the object falling from a distance. Some locals actually saw the object go down into the woods, and to them the object wasn't something out of control and plummeting to the earth. They observed that the object, which passed only a few hundred feet above their heads, was moving very slowly, almost as if it were gliding. One witness said, "It was like some kind of controlled reentry vehicle of some type." It wasn't making any noise, and it looked as though it was trying very carefully not to hit the edge of the mountain ridge. According to these people, that vehicle's crashing caused the blue column of smoke to go up and sent shock waves that were recorded on a seismograph near Detroit.

Stan Gordon, a researcher from the Pennsylvania Association for the Study of the Unexplained who didn't believe the government story, tracked down and questioned several firsthand witnesses, those curious individuals who were actually on the scene. When questioned by Stan they stated that they saw a "copper-bronze colored, saucer-shaped object." The object was between 9 and 12 feet in length and bore a gold band around its bottom with hieroglyphic writing on it. These individuals were quickly removed from the site by the military when they arrived on the scene. Later that night, other witnesses said they observed a flatbed truck carrying a large object covered with a tarpaulin leaving the wooded area. Shortly after the truck's departure, the military personnel vacated the area. Could it have been an alien driver with AAA emergency road service being towed to his local UFO shop via a Pennsylvania highway?

Gordon also found a United States Air Force officer out of Lockbourne in Columbus, Ohio, who was willing to talk. The officer said he was stationed on his base that night. In the wee hours of December 10, 1965, a flatbed truck arrived through the back gates, which were rarely used. He was ordered to patrol the flatbed.

His specific instructions were to shoot anyone who tried to get too close. He was told the truck would be leaving soon for Wright Patterson Air Force Base, which just happens to be the reputed home of other downed UFOs.

Another eyewitness account was from a building contractor who was asked to drop off 6,500 special bricks at a hangar inside Wright Patterson Air Force Base on December 11. Being curious, the builder sneaked a peek in the hangar. He reported seeing several men wearing special white anti-radiation suits who were inspecting a large bell-shaped object, similar in description to the one seen by the witnesses in the woods. Coincidence?

Through additional research Gordon also learned that one of the military groups that was most likely on the scene that night was the 662nd Radar Squadron, based at the Oakdale Armory near the Greater Pittsburgh International Airport. This squadron was used for this covert operation because they were under the control of Aerospace Defense Command. However, when Gordon asked the government about that squadron, they had no record of that squadron or any squadron being activated on that date.

One of the stories circulating was that the object might actually have been Cosmos 96, a Russian probe that was said to have come down over Canada on that same December day. But that possibility was disregarded when both American and

Russian governments denied it. It was further eliminated as a possibility when Nicholas Johnson, a chief scientist at NASA and one of the leading experts in the world on orbital debris and the Russian space system, said, "No way that any debris from Cosmos 96 could have landed in Pennsylvania." In fact according to him, "No other manmade object from any country came down that day."

Yet no one from NASA or the Department of Defense is saying what it was. They're just saying what it's not. And this leaves the Sci-Fi Channel airing their special, "The New Roswell: Kecksburg Exposed," in a very interesting situation. The president of the Sci-Fi Channel, Bonnie Hammer, decided to sue NASA for the information they are not releasing under the Freedom of Information act, stating, "The public has the right to know." As for now, the jury is still out on whether or not the case will go to trial, and still others may be sued depending on the outcome.

And so the mystery continues, with the "real" story being locked away in government files. Was it a meteorite? Was it an alien craft? Was it a government cover-up? Or was it just the overactive imagination of thousands of people? It doesn't seem hard to believe either story; meteorites have fallen to Earth many times before, and as for aliens and government cover-ups, we all know about the stories circulating Roswell, New Mexico. That leaves you, the reader, to decide.

The Mysterious Demise of Dr. Bentley

· 1966 ·

Good ole Doc Bentley was a "horse and buggy" kind of doctor, the type you'd expect to see on an episode of *The Waltons*. He was a practicing physician and surgeon for seventy-one years, and in fact in 1945 Dr. John Irving Bentley had even been honored by the Medical Society of Pennsylvania with a plaque for "fifty years of faithful and loyal service."

Over the course of his career he was a medical examiner for the Selective Services for the local draft board, served as a medical examiner for the German prisoners of war interned at Bark Shanty in WWII, was a physician for the National Youth Center located at Camp Potato, and brought more than 2,000 babies into the world.

In between all that work, he managed to squeeze in three wives and three sons. To those that knew him, he was totally devoted to his career, a fact that some say caused his divorces. He was known to love his work and the people he tended. There were even some folks in the town of Coudersport who could remember when he only charged $1.25 for a house call, and that included the medicine.

So what happened to this beloved doctor on the cold Monday morning of December 5, 1966, that made him the focus not only of a controversial book but also a featured spot on ABC's *That's Incredible?*

Dr. Bentley was in his apartment on that bone-chilling day. He was retired, and since he had suffered a broken hip six years prior and his left leg was without feeling, he made his way about with the aid of a walker, to which was attached a bicycle-type basket. He had hired a woman named Mrs. Nickolson to help with his needs on a part-time basis. On that particular Sunday she had gone into the doctor's house as usual. Her husband stopped by for a while and chatted with the doctor, and both he and Mrs. Nickolson left around 9:00 P.M. That was the last time anyone ever saw or heard from the 92-year-old doctor.

At 9:05 A.M. the next day a North Penn Gas meter reader named Donald Gosnell (who also doubled as a volunteer fireman) opened the door to Dr. Bentley's first-floor apartment to read the meter. He had Dr. Bentley's permission to do this and in fact had done so many times before. He called out a friendly greeting to the doctor but heard no answer. It was a bit odd, but he figured the doctor might have overslept. Nevertheless he walked down the hallway and descended the stairs into the basement where the gas meters were. He noticed a "light blue smoke of unusual odor . . . like that of starting up a new heating system (an oil film burning), somewhat sweet." He walked to the meters and noticed a 5-inch-high pile of ash that was about 14 inches in diameter on the dirt basement floor. By force of fireman's habit, he kicked the ashes and scattered them about. When he saw nothing suspicious, he then went over and read the meter.

On his way out he decided to check in on the doctor to see if he was okay. He peeked his head in the apartment door and noticed the same light blue, sweet-smelling smoke in the doctor's apartment. Gosnell called out to the doctor again, and again there was no answer. He was getting worried now. He went inside and noticed the smoke was also in the living room and bedroom. Gosnell then looked into the bathroom. There he stopped dead in his tracks. "There was a hole about two and a half feet wide and no longer than four feet (that) had burned through the bathroom floor." Pipes were exposed leading to the bathroom and running across the ceiling of the basement. His eyes followed the pipes, and right next to the hole he saw a "browned leg from the knee down—like that of a mannequin. . . . I didn't look further!" Gosnell bolted from the apartment and ran to his gas company office, which was just a few blocks away. He burst into the place screaming, "Dr. Bentley's burnt up!"

John Dec, the deputy coroner for Potter County, described the scene. "All I found was a knee joint, which was atop a post in the basement, the lower leg with its foot on the bathroom floor, and the scattered ashes 6 feet below." Dec commented, "It's funny how one can burn up so completely, and yet not burn the house down. That was the oddest thing I ever saw." This mystery, which was covered in a scant 12 inches in a local newspaper column the following day, became the source of an investigation and a mystery for the town of Coudersport for years to come.

The original hypothesis was rooted in the fact that Dr. Bentley had one big vice: He smoked like a chimney. In fact, it wasn't unusual to see his clothes dotted with burned spots from previous incidents. Originally, people surmised that Dr. Bentley was smoking his pipe and somehow some smoldering tobacco fell into his lap, igniting his robe. It was assumed that, as a result, the doctor hobbled to the bathroom with his walker to get to some water to put the fire out. There was evidence that he struggled hard to save his life because his robe had been removed and was smoldering in the tub, and a broken pitcher of water was found near the remains.

The coroner's report and the scenario reported in the paper at the time left many questions unanswered. For one, witnesses say that Bentley's pipe was in place next to the chair in the living room where he was sitting. If Bentley indeed spilled hot ashes, he wouldn't take the time to carefully place the pipe back while he was on fire. Thus, some in the community believed he had been using a "barn-burner match" (a type of match so big it could burn down a barn) to light his pipe, perhaps dropping the match onto his lap. However, this scenario also raises questions that no one has ever been able to answer, such as why Bentley did not remove his robe immediately instead of waiting to hobble over to the bathroom to get some water.

The most salient point, however, was not addressed by either of these theories. Experienced firemen and many doctors agreed that even if he did wear the burning clothes as he stumbled to the bathroom, the heat would not have been intense enough to cremate a living person. Any fireman will attest that burning clothes could kill a person but not reduce them to ashes. Furthermore, burning clothes do not burn for a long time. The complete disintegration of a body would require temperatures above 3,000 degrees F and involve numerous hours of burning. (Even crematoriums using 3,000 degrees for several hours still have to pulverize bone chips; Dr. Bentley, on the other hand, was pure ash!)

Moreover, experts point out that if the heat from a fire had been intense enough to do that to Dr. Bentley, a kindling point would have been reached and the whole house would have been set ablaze. But the exact opposite happened. There were no signs of burn marks in the house. There weren't even burn marks to a significant degree in the surrounding bathroom area. The only place there was evidence of a fire was where the body once was. Paint on the nearby bathtub was black but not blistered. The rubber tips on Bentley's walker did not even melt, even though they were in direct contact with his body, and his robe was merely smoldering, not burnt. So what the heck happened?

Some investigators believe that the doctor went to the bathroom to relieve the call of nature and that there was a smoldering ash on his robe that he didn't see. Once he noticed it, he took off the robe, put it in the bathtub and went to grab a pitcher of water to put it out. And then, are you ready for this? The doctor spontaneously combusted. Yes, some investigators believe his body simply disintegrated into ashes. Or in more technical terms, "the phenomenon of auto-combustion implies that the burning of an object, in this case a human body, is caused from within, with *no external cause of ignition.*"

This theory of human spontaneous combustion is not new; in fact, many of the world's greatest literary figures, like Mark Twain, Charles Dickens, and Herman Melville, investigated the subject and used case studies as models for victims in their own works. But Dr. Bentley's case is not some writer's novel. This was a real live doctor that just went up in smoke, burning a hole through the bathroom floor in the process and depositing his remains in a pile of ash in the basement. And this rather far-fetched theory is supported by the fact that the house was filled with a sweet smell, not the putrefying smell of burning flesh. This suggests that the entire incident happened very quickly, before the stench could linger in the air. This fact is consistent with other human combustion cases and fits with a pattern that still puzzles scientists since they haven't determined what exactly causes it.

Those who chose to believe the spontaneous combustion theory point to the work of Larry Arnold, a journalist/investigator who authored the book *Ablaze!: The Mysterious Fires of Spontaneous Human Combustion,* as well as other books and articles on this subject. Arnold suggests that "geomagnetic flux," or the mathematical calculation of magnetic activity on the earth, is the reason Dr. Bentley burned up when he did.

According to Arnold, worldwide scientific readings used with precision instruments showed that on the days of December 4 and 5, the magnetic activity of the Earth was high. On a scale of O (quiet) and Z (a storm), it was well near Z, or a peak of 1.1 worldwide, according to mathematical calculations. Therefore the peak in the earth's magnetic activities on December 5, the day of Bentley's death, could have created the optimum conditions for his body to react and spontaneously combust.

Many experts have studied the incident as reported in the paper, examined the coroner's report, looked at the death certificate, and visited the scene of his mysterious demise. The coroner's report has some questionable issues, including the fact the coroner himself admitted he had never seen anything like this, so his report was more of an educated guess. In fact, the "body" was found in a more reduced state than can be accomplished under controlled cremation conditions. Some of the investigators are convinced that Dr. Bentley is just one of the many documented cases of spontaneous combustion. Others prefer to call it a freak accident. Either way, Bentley's apartment still stands today. A new owner took it over and remodeled it. As for what remained of Dr. John Irving Bentley, it is in a grave with a marker in West Hill Cemetery, in Galeton, Potter County.

One thing, though, is certain: The town of Coudersport sadly lost a great physician and gained an unsolved mystery.

Siamese Twins Set a Precedent

· 1977 ·

A new baby's arrival is normally a time of great joy and celebration, and if twins should be born, although twice the work, as some parents know, they are also twice the joy; that is, unless the twins are Siamese. Then a heart-wrenching decision has to be made. And that is precisely what happened at Philadelphia's world-famous Children's Hospital on October 11, 1977. That day a moral precedent was set.

The drama began on September 15 in Lakewood, New Jersey, at a local community hospital when a woman from a prestigious family of Orthodox Jewish Torah educators gave birth to conjoined babies, more popularly referred to as Siamese twins. (The name Siamese comes from the famous twins Chang and Eng Bunker who traveled with Barnum & Bailey circus. They were born in Thailand, formerly known as Siam.)

The Lakewood twins came into the world together with their tiny faces only inches apart. Their color was good, which meant enough oxygen was circulating through both their bodies. Besides being attached, there was only one problem: The duo was joined from the shoulder to the pelvic area.

Later that night Dr. Paul Weinberg, a cardiologist, was summoned from his home to examine an EKG of the twins. He immediately knew something was wrong. As he listened to their chest with a stethoscope, he heard only one heartbeat.

According to the X-rays, Baby B had a normal four-chambered heart that was fused to the stunted two-chambered heart of her sister, Baby A. The hearts were joined along the left ventricles, the main pumping chambers that push the blood through the body. The walls that connected the hearts were too thin to be able to separate them and give each baby the part of the heart that belonged to it. The stunted heart of Baby A would not be able to support her for long. No twins joined at the heart had ever lived for more than nine months. But there was a chance, although slight, that one could be saved if they acted quickly. But an operation this sensitive was not a job for a cardiologist—it was a job for a top surgeon.

Within hours of their birth, the twins (whose names were never released, in keeping with the parents' wishes) were flown by helicopter to Philadelphia to be examined by the best, a man named Dr. C. Everett Koop. Koop, a large, domineering man, had separated conjoined twins twice before. He became a medical star in 1974 when he performed the successful separation of Clara and Alta Rodriquez, who shared a liver, colon, and parts of their intestines. The Rodriquez twins' entire trunks were merged, and their case was considered hopeless. Directing a team of twenty-three surgeons, technicians, and nurses using equipment that he specially designed for the Rodriquez twins, Koop worked painstakingly to separate them. Alta died in a choking incident two years later, but Clara grew to be a healthy adult. The other surgeons were in awe and said it was as if he had worked a miracle, in the true sense of doing something beyond physical law.

So now at this most trying time, the parents of Baby A and Baby B went to this legendary doctor for help. In addition to what Dr. Weinberg had found, Dr. Koop determined that Baby A also had a circulatory defect that would eventually kill her. At that moment the grave truth was confirmed. The one-and-a-half hearts could not sustain both of them; even if they could, Baby A could not survive due to the circulatory defect. If a separation were to be carried out, in the attempt to save Baby B, the life of Baby A would be ended. Those dreadful words echoed throughout the hospital.

Within a few hours of the parents' arrival, a small army of Orthodox rabbis and Talmudic scholars met in the wings to decide the correct action to take. The parents would not make a move without their help and counsel.

It was to become one of the most intense dramas and ethical dilemmas confronting the medical profession, and it was to be played out in the world-famous hospital. No one surgery had provoked more debate, more soul-searching, and more concern about the law than any other surgery in recent years.

Dr. Koop was a deeply religious man, a Presbyterian who had frequently spoken out nationally about the value of human life and about the atrocity of letting newborns with birth defects die. It was ironic that this very doctor might have to perform an operation that would certainly leave one child dead. But if it was to be done, his experience in the field made him the obvious choice to do it. It is rare that a pediatric surgeon ever has to do a Siamese separation, but Koop had done it twice, although he had never separated a shared heart before. Medical professionals watched to see the outcome and knew the horrible situation he was in.

When Dr. Koop examined the twins, even with his strong position on the sanctity of human life, he knew what had to be done. He told the parents. Then the waiting began. The father, a rabbinical student in his mid-twenties, to whom nothing mattered more than God, asked the rabbis if this would be considered murder in the eyes of God.

For eleven nights, the rabbis met for four to five hours discussing the ethical issue. They called in the highly respected Rabbi Moshe Feinstein, the dean of Tifereth Jerusalem Seminary in New York, to help with such a mammoth decision. The big question was, since all human life is considered equal, would it be moral to kill Baby A so that Baby B could live? They discussed the issue among themselves in Hebrew behind closed doors. They needed to examine every possible scenario.

A meeting between the rabbis, the parents, and Dr. Koop was held on September 20 to try to talk about all the options. Another meeting was held three days later.

The clock was ticking as the twins remained in intensive care. Dr. Koop felt time was running out. At any moment the twin's heart could fail and both babies would die. As horrible as it was, Dr. Koop and many other members of the medical community believed that separating the twins was the lesser of two evils, and it needed to be done as soon as possible. With surgery, at least there was a theoretical chance one could be saved. Without surgery there was no hope.

The clock kept ticking. The parents prayed. The rabbis talked. The doctors waited.

The issue was not easy for anyone, including some of the hospital staff. Many of the Catholic nurses consulted their local priests. The priests advised them. Their argument was: "God expects us to act when we can act. Not to choose is to choose to allow both of the babies to die. It was not the doctors who would be killing the baby, because they would save the girl if they could, but the terminal event that had already started for her." Many were comforted, but in the end two Catholic nurses and three anesthesiologists asked not to be assigned to the surgery.

The clock still ticked.

It was Friday and it was getting late. The rabbis needed to get home before sundown, the beginning of the Sabbath.

The surgeons, cardiologists, and all medical personnel were becoming increasingly worried that the surgery was being delayed too long. It would take time to put together the elaborate team of doctors that was needed for this operation. Dr. Koop decided to assemble a team just in case. If the parents decided to go ahead with the surgery, they could act right away. If the parents decided not to, the worst that would happen was that professional time would be lost.

On September 30, twenty nurses and doctors assembled to discuss the case and all the unknowns, of which there were many. When a surgeon prepares to do heart surgery, he usually has a good idea of what the heart will look like. In this case, Dr. Henry Edmunds, the chairman of cardiothoracic surgery, had no idea. This made him extremely uneasy. He could not examine the heart once he started surgery. Time was of the essence.

Dr. Weinberg's X-ray only showed parts of the heart chambers, enough to determine that there were six. But it did not show the vital information that was needed for surgery, such as how much blood was going into the heart muscle. Edmund needed this information to know when to tie off any blood vessels and separate the normal four-chambered heart from the stunted two. The only alternative was to put the entire six-chambered heart inside the tiny chest of Baby B, but to do so they would have to build up the size of Baby B's chest cavity using ribs from Baby A.

The meeting went on for hours, with the surgeons working out strategies to overcome every potential problem.

The team of doctors decided that if needed, they could do the surgery as early as October 11. Hopefully the rabbis would come to the decision at the same time.

On October 3, the intensive care nurses saw a change in the babies' EKG: Baby A's heart was failing. They administered digitalis, a drug used to strengthen the heart.

On October 6, only five days before the tentative surgery was scheduled, the rabbis decided in favor of the surgery and the father agreed to it. They felt that since one twin's life was clearly going to be brief, while the other twin's life could potentially be full and healthy, that Baby A was endangering Baby B's life. Even if the harm was unintentional, they could be separated in accordance with Jewish law.

The family requested that Baby A be returned home for burial before sundown after the surgery. Dr. Koop gave his assurance that he would arrange it.

The final planning session for surgery was on October 7.

On October 10, Columbus Day, a day when the courts are normally closed, three judges met with Dr. Koop and his lawyers in family court. The lawyers presented their case to the judges following the same reasoning as the rabbis. The court decided because there is a greater good served by saving one child instead of losing both, the court would be justified in issuing an order.

Surgery was scheduled for 6:00 A.M. on October 11. The cold, black day reflected the mood of all at the hospital. At 6:05 a voice yelled, "They're here." All faces in the brightly lit surgery room turned to see the two tiny twins. The intensive care nurses were crying, knowing it would be the last time they would see Baby A. The babies were put to sleep immediately with nitrous oxide, and then the surgery began.

Four hours into the surgery, the oxygen level of the blood in the twins dropped dangerously low, even with all the care the anesthesiologist was giving. All they could do was hope and pray. Eventually the major blood vessels were isolated and sutures were tied around them, ready to be cut off simultaneously on signal. This was the most difficult part of the surgery. It had to be done at precisely the right moment or poisons from Baby A's blood would start pouring into the blood of Baby B the moment Baby A died. These poisons would shut down the healthy heart.

At 10:40 Dr. Koop gave the signal and he personally tied off the carotid artery, which was Baby A's lifeline. He felt it was his duty to do it. Death was instantaneous.

Everyone watched the monitors. Was Baby B okay? For a moment nothing happened, then like a miracle the oxygen level in the blood improved. A force greater than them was on their side. There were no grafts, no cutting, nothing that needed to be done around the heart. All the tissues from the heart and lungs were separated. And nothing further was needed to be taken from Baby A. Baby B's chest was expanded, and the heart was beating strong and well. She was wheeled back to intensive care in stable but critical condition.

Baby A was sent home in a speeding vehicle so her body could be laid to rest before sundown. Baby B went home, but lived for only three months before she died of liver failure and an overwhelming infection.

A few hours after Baby A's memorial, a very solemn press conference was conducted with all questions answered. The final words came from Dr. Koop, who said, "This was the hardest day of my professional life, but only because of what I had to do, not for moral reasons. The morals of the situation were clear. We had to choose between two deaths, or one death and one life. We chose life."

Thirty Minutes
to Meltdown
· 1979 ·

Everyone fears nuclear accidents, but not everyone knows how easy it is for an accident to occur. It's so easy, in fact, that something as simple as a small leak that produces the same volume equal to a glassful of water could trigger a chain of events that leads to a major disaster. And that's exactly what happened near Harrisburg, Pennsylvania, on March 28, 1979, at the Three Mile Island nuclear power plant.

Chernobyl was the worst nuclear accident known to the civilized world. But the largest to occur in the United States was Three Mile Island or TMI, as it was nicknamed. This power plant was built in two parts: TMI-1, a gigantic 800-megawatt reactor that started operating in September of 1974, and TMI-2, its bigger brother, a 900-megawatt, pressurized, 100-ton water reactor, which began operating four years later. At full capacity they could together produce enough energy to light 18,000 homes. These reactors sat on one of the islands along the Susquehanna River in south-central Pennsylvania.

Just three short months after TMI-2 was in service, the nearby residents were awakened at 4:00 A.M. by a terrible roar. This was not the first time that the reactor let out a bellow, but it was the first time it occurred at such an ungodly hour.

Bill Whittock, a retired civil engineer, remembers seeing a huge cloud of steam jetting out of TMI-2's containment building.

After looking at the spectacle for a few minutes, he went back to bed. In fact, that was the reaction of most residents. Like people who live near a volcano, they got used to the rumbling, while in the back of their minds they knew that one day it could possibly explode. But no one had reason to believe this would be the day.

In a pressurized water reactor (PWR) like TMI-2, uranium, a highly radioactive substance, is used to create heat. Heat is used to boil the water and turn it into steam. A carefully controlled chain reaction occurs, and massive amounts of energy are released. Since the radioactive material is harmful, the container that it is stored in includes a complex two-loop cooling system to keep it safe. In case of leakage, the first line of defense is the first loop. If it isn't caught there, its leakage is caught in the second loop. This two-loop system must be kept under an extremely careful watch.

That morning, about an hour before the roar occurred, the third-shift foreman, Fred Scheimann, and two operators were in TMI-2 in the secondary loop area. The trio was trying to clean a jammed polisher, which filters the impurities out of the feeding water. The polisher had jammed many times before and usually they were able to flush it out right away. But this morning the normal method of blasting beads into the blocked pipe in the polisher to clear it out wasn't working. Instead, Scheimann agitated the water in the bottom of the polisher. It created a mixture of air, water, and resin, which bubbled up and finally popped the blockage out of the pipe.

However, in fixing this problem they created a small leak in the system. The leak caused a slight change in the air pressure, which caused the system to detect an interruption to the normal flow. The interruption set the emergency backup and safety systems into action and the pumps shut down. When the effect reached the reactor core, the chain reaction stopped. A control valve released the steam that normally would have been used to generate electricity into the outside air. That release is what caused the roar heard by the residents.

At that point no one realized that the blast was the first sign of an unprecedented nuclear disaster. Everything in the system was shutting down as expected. Everything except for the Electromatic Relief Valve (ERV), a very important valve that maintains the cooling systems pressure and water levels. The ERV valve (which had malfunctioned eleven times before in other nuclear plants but was never modified) was supposed to remain open for only thirteen seconds in this type of situation. Instead it stayed open, allowing the highly radioactive primary coolant to continue to pour from the reactor core into the holding tank at a rate of 200 gallons per minute. The problem, however, was that the control panel indicated the ERV had closed properly. Why? Because the panel was only designed to indicate the last command given to the ERV valve, not that it needed to be closed.

In the meantime, the temperature in the core began to rise at a rate of 40 degrees F per second. The steam generators began to boil dry, and the backup pumps couldn't work because their valves were closed.

The shift supervisor, Bill Zewe, warned the workers over the loudspeaker that they were in the first stage of an emergency. Then Zewe and two expert operators, Craig Faust and Ed Frederick, began to study the 40-foot-long, complex instrument control board, which consisted of thousands of buttons that monitored everything that went on in the plant. They desperately went down a checklist, button by button, to find the problem.

The control board indicated that the backup emergency pumps (also known as the "twelves" because they were number 12A & 12B on the checklist) were working at full speed. What Faust didn't know was that two days prior, during a routine testing, a maintenance worker broke one of the strictest requirements of the NRC and shut off the backup water feeder flow by closing the pumps' block valves. This was *never* to be done without a complete shut down of the reactor. The problem was that after the inspection, the maintenance worker had forgotten to reopen them. To make matters worse, a maintenance tag attached to a nearby switch on the control board was obscuring one of the lights. Faust assumed the twelves were opened and the pumps were working fine because the other emergency indicator lights said they were on. Had Faust seen the lights behind the tag he would have known they weren't on.

It was now 4:07 A.M., only seven minutes since that roar occurred. If at this very moment they had discovered that the ERV valve was open, they could have saved TMI-2. Instead a design flaw in the control board made them think that the reactor had too much coolant, when in fact the exact opposite was true: They had too little. In an effort to correct what they erroneously thought was "the problem," Frederick shut down the high-pressure pumps, cutting down any water that was leaking to the pumps. That was the worst possible thing to do. Now the reactor would heat up even faster and at this rate cause a meltdown in thirty minutes.

As soon as Frederick executed his move, the board showed that they had high temperatures and low pressure, yet they knew they were fully pressurized. As they were trying to figure out what was going on, Faust noticed the lights underneath the tag. He screamed, "THE TWELVES ARE CLOSED!" and quickly flicked the switch, restoring water to the emergency feedwater pumps. Immediately the secondary loop filled with coolant and drew some heat away from the reactor. But it was too late. The two steam generators were now damaged from the intense heat, and only one was able to pump water.

It was now 4:14 A.M. Another loud alarm went off. This time the signal indicated that the holding tank had burst, spilling one-quarter of a million gallons of boiling radioactive coolant onto the concrete floor of the containment building.

Suddenly more than one hundred alarms blared loudly, and the computer started spurting out hundreds of pages of warnings, but the most important warning, the one that would indicate that the ERV was still open, did not print out until three hours later.

By 4:40 A.M., operators realized that the primary coolant that had drained from the reactor into the auxiliary building was radioactive. They quickly vacated and sealed off the building. Unfortunately, the gas from the auxiliary building had already escaped through the ventilation system. Radioactivity was now in the outside air and could affect the people in the surrounding area.

By 5:00, the reactor core started to boil dry. The pumps began to vibrate violently. They had to shut down the entire cooling system.

Between 5:20 and 6:15, the reactor core reached lavalike temperatures of 5,000 degrees F. The system was at the beginning of a meltdown.

At 6:22, the operators finally discovered the ERV was opened. They closed the valve two hours and twenty-two minutes after the first sign of trouble. Just before 7:00, Zewe decided to declare a site emergency. It is estimated that those residents by the shore of the Susquehanna River were possibly being exposed to ten rems per hour. The average American is exposed to just .2 rems of radiation per year (and that's throwing in a medical X-ray). The reactor was leaking 800 rems per hour, and yet the control panel still did not indicate that two-thirds of the core was exposed.

At 7:24, Zewe changed the status to a general emergency. In the history of the commercial nuclear plant industry, no one ever had declared a general emergency. Governor Dick Thornburgh, local police, and the fire department were alerted, as well as the plant owner, Metropolitan Edison (Met Ed). The PEMA (Pennsylvania Emergency Management Council) advised the Civil Defense to be prepared to evacuate the area of Goldsboro and Brunner Island, west of TMI.

At 8:25, a local news director at WKBO radio, Mike Pintek, got wind of the situation from a CB radio. Pintek went on the air mentioning the state of emergency over at the plant. It was the world's first hint that one of the worst nuclear accidents in history had begun.

The nightmare continued to grow. Another operator opened the motorized blocking valve on the pressurizer, causing more coolant to leave the reactor. In the process, a hydrogen bubble formed at the top of the reactor core. Two nuclear experts started arguing about how dangerous the bubble was.

In an effort to keep the public calm, Lieutenant Governor Bill Scranton held a press conference at 11:00 saying there was "no danger to public health and safety" from the situation at TMI. By 4:00 P.M., he had to eat those words. The hydrogen bubble had ignited, releasing more radioactivity into the environment.

Officials worked through the night trying to fix the problem. Residents were naturally upset and sat glued to their radio and television sets, waiting for word of evacuation. On Thursday, March 29, more press conferences were held. Met Ed, the plant owner, denied any danger to the public. The governor also kept reassuring the people that there was "no cause for alarm."

With so many agencies now involved, a series of miscommunications were set in motion. The plant owners were announcing to the public that there was no danger, while government officials were prescribing safety measures. By 10:00 A.M. on Friday, the governor urged everyone within a 10-mile radius of the plant to stay indoors until further notice. Schools were told to keep children inside during recess, and people were told to stay off the phone lines so as not to jam the system.

At 11:15 A.M., the air sirens went off in Harrisburg. To this day, they do not know who set the alarm. No official evacuation orders were in place, but the blaring sirens naturally panicked an already troubled neighborhood and some began to flee.

By 12:30 P.M., Governor Thornburgh advised the pregnant women and preschool children within a 5-mile radius to evacuate. A mass exodus of 140,000 people began. People threw things in their cars and left. Others withdrew all their money from the bank and safety deposit boxes. With the panic, phone lines were tied up, the roads were jammed, and not one single community near Three Mile Island had thought to make up an extensive evacuation plan.

President Jimmy Carter went on the air to calm public fears: "If a full evacuation is necessary your governor will ask you and others in the area to take appropriate actions to ensure your safety . . . this will not indicate that the danger level is high, it will indicate that a change is being made in the operation of the cooling water system to permanently correct the present state of the reactor, and it is strictly a precautionary measure." The hydrogen bubble itself must have been listening, because by Monday, April 2, the bubble shrank to 175 cubic feet, and no evacuation was ordered. Friday, March 30, went down in Pennsylvanian history as "Black Friday."

Today, the TMI-2 reactor is permanently shut down and defueled. The reactor coolant system is drained, the radioactive water has been decontaminated and evaporated, the radioactive waste was shipped to an appropriate disposal site, and the reactor fuel and core debris were shipped to a Department of Energy facility. The remainder of the site is constantly monitored.

Ironically the taxpayers are still paying for not only the cleanup of the catastrophe but also the cost of the building of the reactor in the first place. Luckily no one died that day, but we do not yet know the long-term effects of the radiation leak.

As a result of the TMI disaster, which was a combination of miscommunication, poor equipment, and human error, in 1979 the nuclear energy industry created a self-governing body called the Nuclear Power Operations, to address public safety issues and to keep a watchful eye on nuclear power plants.

Heroes in the Sky

• 2001 •

At 10:37 A.M. on Tuesday, September 11, 2001, United Airlines Flight 93 crashed into the ground in Somerset County near the small town of Shanksville, Pennsylvania. There were no survivors. No one on the ground was injured. It is nearly impossible to fathom that on this particular day, this one fact was as close as we would come to good news. If it were not for the heroic efforts of the innocent passengers on this flight, the number of lives lost on September 11 would have been significantly higher.

It was one of the darkest days in the history of the planet; the terrorist attacks that occurred on 9/11 rocked the world. Nearly everyone everywhere was affected directly or indirectly by the events brought about by a man named Osama Bin Laden and his al-Qaeda terrorism network.

It is now known that Bin Laden organized at least nineteen terrorists to hijack four different aircraft. Once under the control of the hijackers, each plane had a specific mission of death and destruction. The first two flying bombs targeted the World Trade Center towers in New York City. A third was directed at the Pentagon in Washington, D.C. While the ultimate destination of the fourth flight will never be known, it is assumed the hijackers of this plane also had designs on the Washington, D.C., area, based on the route the plane was taking when it went down.

United Flight 93 had departed from Newark, New Jersey, and was en route to San Francisco, California, when the crew was overpowered and lost control of their craft, somewhere near Cleveland, Ohio. The four terrorists dramatically changed the route of the Boeing 757 southwest toward Pittsburgh. Radar showed that the plane began to lose altitude and was being flown erratically. The passengers were aware of the hijacking of their own plane but completely unaware of the events occurring in New York and Washington.

The tense situation must have been overwhelming. It is unlikely that the passengers and crew could imagine the grave purpose of their captors' assignment, but living in the information age, several of the passengers made phone calls from the airplane to family and friends on the ground. By this time, the whole country was aware of the mayhem in New York and Washington. Word quickly spread through the airplane, and with a sense of doom, everyone aboard began to understand his or her fate.

One passenger, Todd Beamer, was a 32-year-old businessman and Sunday school teacher, as well as a husband and father to two young boys. Todd used the credit-card operated air phone to call in the emergency situation. Todd was connected to an operator from GTE named Lisa Jefferson. They spent a total of thirteen minutes in conversation. Mr. Beamer gave a detailed account of what was happening on the airplane, and Ms. Jefferson described the attacks on the World Trade Center and the Pentagon.

Todd Beamer's call was placed at 9:45 A.M. He told Lisa Jefferson that there were four hijackers, three of whom had knives while the fourth had what looked like a bomb tied with a red sash or belt to his upper body. He explained that the man with the apparent bomb stayed near the rear of the plane while two others took over the cockpit, forcibly removing the pilot and copilot and locking the door behind them. It is not clear what position the fourth hijacker took.

In the process of exchanging this information, Todd and a number of his fellow travelers put together a hasty plan to thwart the four terrorists. Todd then asked Lisa Jefferson to pray with him, and together they recited Psalm 23. Next Todd asked her to promise to phone his wife, also named Lisa, and his sons, David and Andrew.

The other passengers who made calls from the airplane all called loved ones. Their names were Thomas Burnett, 38; Jeremy Glick, 31; and Mark Bingham, also 31. Both Burnett and Glick conveyed that they were going to try to do something.

Meanwhile, the rest of the country was not holding still. President George W. Bush ordered the military to intercept and shoot down any commercial airliners that refused to turn away from Washington or any other "target of opportunity." Despite the obvious need for such an order, it was a painful decision to make. Shooting down an airplane full of innocent citizens creates multiple problems, not the least of which is possible collateral damage on the ground.

Thankfully, this option became unnecessary due to the efforts of the brave souls aboard United Flight 93. The heroes knew instinctively that they were the best last defense for their country. It would have also been their only hope of survival. Maybe they would get lucky and take back control of the aircraft.

When Todd Beamer finished his prayer and secured Jefferson's promise to call his wife, he put the phone down, leaving the line still connected to GTE. That is when Lisa Jefferson heard Todd's last words: "Let's roll."

What followed was pure mayhem. While the details will never be known, it is assumed that various passengers attacked the various terrorists at the same time. Certainly someone broke down the cabin door and rushed the hijackers manning the controls. Officials have stated that it appears the hijackers put the craft into an irreversible dive, causing United Flight 93 to crash in an empty field.

While so few details are available about the actual methods used, the end result was there for all to see. The mission of United Flight 93's brave passengers was a success. Not one person on the ground was injured or killed and the monstrous hijackers of at least this one plane failed to complete their objective. On a day with very few bright moments, this valiant effort by the common man stands out as a true highlight.

By Friday of that week, GTE operator Lisa Jefferson received permission and clearance to contact Mr. Beamer's wife to pass on Todd's last-minute sentiments. Lisa Beamer later stated, "People asked me if I'm upset that I didn't speak with him [Todd], but I'm glad he called [Jefferson] instead. I would have been helpless. And I know what his last words would have been to me, anyway. I think that's why he chose the method he did."

David Beamer, Todd's father, was quoted at his memorial service as saying, "We know why he was on it [United Flight 93]. The faces of evil—those particular hijackers—they got on the wrong plane."

Pennsylvania Governor Tom Ridge, who would soon be appointed director of the newly formed Department of Homeland Security, attended a vigil outside the Somerset County Courthouse. In his remarks he stated, "The passengers on that plane decided to fight back their hijackers. They undoubtedly saved hundreds, if not thousands, of lives in the process. They sacrificed themselves for others, the ultimate sacrifice."

Ridge, who earlier had visited the crash site, went on to say, "What appears to be a charred, smoldering hole in the ground is truly and really a monument to heroism."

Many flowery words have been heaped upon these courageous passengers who refused to be victims. Political and religious leaders at every level of importance to our country have stepped forward to commend and memorialize them. Perhaps the most fitting eulogy is the simple final phrase of Todd Beamer: "Let's roll."

•

A Potpourri of Pennsylvania Facts

Bare Facts about Pennsylvania:

The state animal is the white-tailed deer.

The state flower is the mountain laurel.

The state tree is the hemlock.

The state fish is the brook trout.

The state bird is the ruffed grouse.

The state insect is the firefly.

The state dog is the Great Dane.

The state capital is Harrisburg.

The state nicknames are the Keystone State and Quaker State.

• People have resided in Pennsylvania since 10,000 B.C.

• Pennsylvania is one of four commonwealths (the others are Virginia, Massachusetts, and Kentucky).

• Pennsylvania covers an area of 46,055 square miles.

• Pennsylvania became the second state on December 12, 1787.

• Pennsylvania borders six other states (New York, New Jersey, Delaware, Maryland, West Virginia, and Ohio).

• The only president from Pennsylvania was James Buchanan.

• Pennsylvania means "Penn's Woods."

• Hannah Penn was Pennsylvania's only female governor to date.

- Pennsylvania is the state with the most covered bridges, also known as "kissin' bridges."

- The oldest street in Pennsylvania is Elfreth's Alley in Philadelphia.

- Pennsylvania has seven professional sports teams. In Pittsburgh the teams are the Steelers (football), Pirates (baseball), and Penguins (hockey). In Philadelphia they are the Eagles (football), Phillies (baseball), Flyers (hockey), and 76ers (basketball).

- The Pennsylvania Dutch aren't Dutch at all; their ancestors came from Germany and Switzerland. They spoke *Deutsch,* but the English-speaking settlers misunderstood and called them Dutch.

- Lancaster was the capital of the United States for one day.

- Pennsylvania is the birthplace of cable TV and HBO.

- Driving on the right side of the road originated in Pennsylvania.

- The printed ballot was introduced in Pennsylvania under the election law in 1799.

- A Pennsylvanian by the name of Charles Darrow invented the famous board game Monopoly.

- The Hershey "Kiss" candy is named for the sound made during production.

- The Please Touch Museum in Philadelphia was the nation's first museum for children age seven and under.

- In 1907 Irvin and Claree Scott of Philadelphia invented paper towels.

- Benjamin Franklin started the first library in the colonies in 1731.

- The first U.S. commercial railroad began running in Pennsylvania in 1829.

- Pennsylvanian Christopher L. Sholes invented the typewriter.

- KDKA in Pittsburgh was the country's first radio station.

- The first World Series was played in Pittsburgh in 1903.

- Hershey's is the world's largest chocolate factory.

- Little League baseball began in Williamsport.

- The first Girl Scout cookie sale took place in 1933 in Philadelphia.

- Pennsylvania was the first state to pass a law abolishing slavery, abolition law, a minimum wage law, and a compulsory school attendance law.

- Joshua Pusey invented a book of matches in 1889 in Middletown.

Famous Pennsylvanians: John James Audubon, Louisa May Alcott, Marian Anderson, Stephen Foster, Daniel Boone, Rachel Carson, Mary Cassatt, Wilt Chamberlain, Bill Cosby, W. C. Fields, Benjamin Franklin, Grace Kelly, Arnold Palmer, Fred Rogers, Andrew Wyeth, Michael Keaton, Patti LaBelle, Reggie Jackson, Joe Montana, Jim Thorpe, Andrew Carnegie, Nellie Bly, Chubby Checkers, Lloyd Alexander, Jerry Spinelli, Dennis Miller, Tom Ridge, Man Ray, Joe Namath, Johnny Unitas, Gene Kelly, Sharon Stone, George Blanda, Orrin Hatch, Newt Gingrich, Dan Marino, Jim Kelly, Johnny Weismuller, Charles Bronson, Jack Palance, Franco Harris, Jimmy Stewart, Andy Warhol.

Bibliography and Further Reading

Books

Baseball Encyclopedia, The. Macmillan/Simon and Schuster, 1996.

Bimba, Anthony. *The Molly Maguires: The True Story of Labor's Martyred Pioneers in the Coalfields.* New York: International Publishers, 1950.

Boland, Charles Michael. *Ring in the Jubilee: The Epic of America's Liberty Bell.* Riverside, Connecticut: Chatham Press, 1973.

Chidsey, Donald Barr. *Lewis and Clark: The Great Adventure.* New York: Crown Publishers, 1970.

Clark, J. Stanley. *The Oil Century.* Norman: University of Oklahoma Press, 1958.

Couch, Ernie and Jill. *Pennsylvania Trivia.* Nashville: Rutledge Hill Press, 1988.

Cummings, Hubertis. *The Mason and Dixon Line: Story for a Bicentenary 1763-1963.* Department of Internal Affairs, Commonwealth of Pennsylvania, 1962.

Davis, Devra. *When Smoke Ran Like Water: Tales of Environmental Deception and the Battle Against Pollution.* New York: Basic Books, 2002.

Dewees, F. P. *The Molly Maguires: The Origin, Growth, and Character of the Organization.* New York: Burt Franklin, 1877.

Duncan, Dayton and Ken Burns. *Lewis & Clark: The Journey of the Corps of Discovery; An Illustrated History.* New York: Knopf, 1997.

Esposito, Jackie and Steven Herb. *The Nittany Lion: An Illustrated Tale.* University Park, Pennsylvania: Pennsylvania State University Press, 1997.

Frear, Ned. *The Lost Children.* Bedford County Visitors Bureau.

Garrison, Webb. *A Treasury Of Pennsylvania Tales.* Nashville: Rutledge Hill Press, 1996.

Graeff, Arthur D. *It Happened In Pennsylvania.* Philadelphia: The John C. Winston Company, 1947.

Harry, Lou. *Strange Philadelphia: Stories from the City of Brotherly Love.* Philadelphia: Temple University Press, 1995.

Jones, Penelope Redd. *The Story Of The Pennsylvania Turnpike.* Mechanicsburg, PA: Camelot Farms, c.1950.

Kantor, MacKinlay. *Gettysburg.* New York: Random House, 1952.

Lewis, Arthur H. *Lament For The Molly Maguires.* New York: Harcourt, Brace, and World, 1964.

Liljegren, S. B. *The Irish Element in the Valley of Fear.* Irish Institute, Uppsala University, 1964.

Longman, Jere. *Among the Heroes.* New York: HarperCollins, 2002.

McCullough, David. *The Johnstown Flood.* New York: Simon and Schuster, 1968.

Miller, Natalie. *The Story of the Liberty Bell.* Chicago: Children's Press, 1965.

Miller, Randall M., and William Pencak, eds. *Pennsylvania: A History of the Commonwealth*. University Park: Pennsylvania State University Press, 2002.

O'Connor, Richard. *Johnstown: The Day the Dam Broke*. Philadelphia: Lippincott, c.1957.

Peterson, Helen Stone. *Give Us Liberty! The Story of the Declaration of Independence*. Champaign, Ill.: Garrard Publishing Company, 1973.

Plunkett-Powell, Karen. *Remembering Woolworth's*. New York: Saint Martin's Press, 1999.

Rogers, Frances and Alice Beard. *The Old Liberty Bell*. Philadelphia: Lippincott, 1942.

Rosewater, Victor. *The Liberty Bell: Its History and Significance*. New York and London: D. Appleton and Company, 1926.

Schneck, Marcus. *Country Towns of Pennsylvania*. 2nd ed. Country Roads Press, 2000.

Shank, William H. *Vanderbilt's Folly: A History of the Pennsylvania Turnpike*. York, Pennsylvania: American Canal and Transportation Center, 1973.

Shook, Robert L. *Why Didn't I Think of That!* New York: The New American Library, 1982.

Storrick, W. C. *Gettysburg: The Place, the Battles, the Outcome*. New York: Barnes and Noble, 1993.

Swain, Gwenyth. *Pennsylvania*. Hello U.S.A. Minneapolis: Lerner Publications Company, 2002.

Wallace, Anthony F. C. *King of the Delawares: Teedyuscung, 1700–1763*. Freeport, NY: Books for Libraries Press, 1949.

Yoder, Don. *Groundhog Day*. Mechanicsburg, Pennsylvania: Stackpole Books, 2003.

Newspapers

Donald C. Drake, "Siamese Twins: The Surgery; An Agonizing Choice—Parents, Doctors, Rabbis in Dilemma," *Philadelphia Inquirer,* 16 October 1977.

Edward J. Gerrity, "This is My Town: Price-Pancoast Disaster," *Scranton Times,* 9 July 1967.

"Pancoast Mine Map: Courtesy of Pennsylvania Anthracite Museum at McDade Park, Scranton," *Tribune-Republican,* 8 April 1911.

"Sixty-Two Die in Throop Mine Fire," *Tribune-Republican,* 8 April 1911.

Journals and Magazines

"Found Cremated in Home, County's Oldest Physician Dies," *Potter County Journal,* 8 December 1966.

Moffett, Cleveland. "The Overthrow of the Molly Maguires—Stories from the Archives of the Pinkerton Detective Agency." *McClure's Magazine,* vol. 4, 1894–1895, 90–100.

"Oldest Practicing Physician in Potter County," *Potter County Times,* vol. 107 no. 5, 30 June 1955.

Pursuit—The Journal of the Society for the Investigation of the Unexplained, vol. 9 no. 4, 1976.

"Transcript from Council Held at Philadelphia ye 21st of ye 12th Month, 1683," Provincial Council from the Pennsylvania Colonial Records, vol. 1.

Index

About the Authors

Fran Capo is a highly energetic and humorous stand-up comic, voice-over artist, spokesperson, adventurer, freelance writer, and keynote motivational speaker for Fortune 500 companies. In addition to this book, Fran has authored seven others: *How to Get Publicity Without a Publicist, How to Break into Voiceovers, Humor in Business Speaking, It Happened in New York, It Happened in New Jersey, Almost a Wise Guy,* and *Adrenaline Adventures.* She has also co-created the award-winning cyber-sitcom *The Estrogen Files: Money, Men and Motherhood* at www.TheEstrogenFiles.net.

Fran is also recorded in the *Guinness Book of World Records* as the Fastest Talking Female. She was clocked at 603.32 wpm and has been featured on over two dozen commercials. This Queens College graduate has been on over 1,000 radio shows and 250 television programs, including *Larry King Live, Entertainment Tonight, Ripley's Believe it or Not, Last Call with Carson Daly, Inside Edition, Good Morning America, The Today Show, Fox News Live,* and *ESPN2 Cold Pizza.*

Fran has also been featured in numerous books, including *Chicken Soup for the Woman's Soul, The Book of Wisdom, Comic Lives, Life's a Stitch, Become a Recognized Authority in Your Field, My Word,* and *Revolutionary Laughter.* As an adventurer she has bungee jumped, walked on hot coals, and dived with sharks, all of which you can read about in her book, *Adrenaline Adventures.* Fran is the proud mother of Spencer Patterson, an all-around great kid and the world's youngest comic and ventriloquist. To learn more about Fran Capo or have her speak for your organization, visit her Web site www.francapo.com or reach her by e-mail at FranCNY@aol.com.

Scott Bruce is a nationally touring headline comedian as well as the host of the Emmy-award winning PBS television show *The Pennsylvania Game*. He has appeared on many national and local television and radio shows. He also writes, produces, and appears as the talent for many radio and television commercials. Scott and his wife Anne own and operate Wise Crackers Comedy Clubs, which are located throughout Pennsylvania.

Scott is the host of other touring game shows, such as "The Rules Of The Game," a sports trivia game, and "The 80s Game," a trivia game not surprisingly about the 1980s. He has also created new game shows including *FLOG,* a TV game show about golf, and "Quirky Quotations," a game show featuring humorous quotes from famous people, which is currently running on a number of radio programs.

A bona fide Macintosh computer geek, Scott is also a notoriously mediocre golfer. He and wife Anne are the proud parents of Nicholas and Chloe. They live almost like a normal family in the Pocono Mountains of Pennsylvania. To learn more about Scott, his upcoming appearances, or Wise Crackers Comedy Clubs, visit www.wisecrackers.biz or e-mail him at scottbruce@aol.com.